Rewire Your Anxious Brain to Fix
Thoughts and Disco

LETTING GO OF

OVERTHINKING
IN
RELATIONSHIPS
AND
RELATIONSHIPS
ANXIETY

WORKBOOK

ROBERT J. CHARLES, PHD, DMIN

Letting Go of Overthinking in Relationships and Relationships Anxiety Workbook

Rewire Your Anxious Brain to Fix an Unhealthy Relationship, Stop Toxic Thoughts and Discover Your Attachment Style

By Robert J. Charles, PhD, DMin

Contents

Breathtaking BONUS! #1

Master the Art of Building Stronger Bonds with Loves Ones

In this Bonus, you'll find:

- How to Develop Effective Communication Strategies
- Ways to Build a Healthy Relationship Plan
- Exercises to Establish Healthy Boundaries for Personal Growth

Discover Powerful Strategies to Elevate Your Relationships to New Heights!
<u>Click here to get this BONUS.</u>

Amazing BONUS! #2

Companion Worksheets

<u>7 Transformative Worksheets</u> for Cultivating a New Mindset for a Better Life

Inside this BONUS, you'll discover:

- How to Cultivate Self-Compassion for True Happiness?
- How to Unleash Your Happy Hormones?
- How to Create Your Ideal Self-Care Routine?

If you want to start a better life with self-compassion and self-care

<u>Download this BONUS.</u>

Join Our Facebook Support Group

Join our affectionate community of *Anxiety, Depression, and Emotional Regulation Support Group* on Facebook. You will be able to connect and share tips and strategies with other like-minded people. If you want to achieve your goals, don't take this journey alone.

It would be great to connect with you there!

>> Click Here to Join our Anxiety, Depression, and Emotional Regulation Support Group <<

Introduction

"I know you guys are close but does he have to come everywhere with us?"

Selena had always been a kind and thoughtful partner, but her relationships were often plagued by worry and overthinking. Even when she was happy, her mind was always racing with worries and fears, especially the fear of becoming vulnerable and ending up hurt. One day, her partner, Alex, organized a surprise picnic by the lake. Selena's thoughts ran wild and began to race with questions as they sat together: "Does he really love me? What happens if something goes wrong? Is he trying to break up with me?"

Alex, sensing her discomfort, moved closer to her and took her hands in his. "You know, Selena, I've come to realize that our mind can be both our biggest ally and our most cruel critic. It has the power to make up situations that aren't grounded in reality. But if we allow this, we risk missing out on the beauty and genuineness of our relationship. I want us to be present in this moment, free from the shackles of overthinking." Selena saw that her overthinking was robbing her of beautiful moments with Alex, so she made a conscious effort to let go of her anxieties and live in the present.

Falling and being in love, as you've probably noticed, is not quite the same in reality as it is portrayed in the movies. It's messy and complicated, and the scene where you stand in the rain and blurt out your feelings to each other and then hug passionately definitely never happens. Relationships are like intricate dances that require the complete focus, patience, and dedication of both partners. Like we've all heard so many times, love is a choice. It takes time and effort. And while it might seem beautiful and rosy at the start of the relationship, it rarely stays that way for too long.

The end of a relationship also is never painless, especially if you've been treated unfairly throughout the relationship. As someone who has experienced what it feels like to be abused and taken advantage of, I know how much it hurts to let somebody go or be let go of regardless of if the person was right for me or not. And I know how much this can affect future relationships.

It might seem unfair and irrational, but projecting the fears and anxiety earned from a previous relationship is bound to occur, and if not properly addressed can cause a lot of problems in the current relationship and could even lead to the death of the relationship.

Allowing overthinking and anxiety to cast a cloud over your relationship doesn't always stem from the wounds sustained from a previous relationship, though; it can occur as a result of dysfunctions in how you were raised and the home you grew up in, or as part of a personality trait you just can't seem to shed. One thing, however, is certain: overthinking and anxiety make it difficult to find happiness and peace.

Knowing this, however, doesn't automatically make things better. I learned this the hard way when I realized that I was clinging to my anxiety and overthinking to avoid facing and working on them. Sounds weird, doesn't it? Shouldn't the fact that I understood the problem have made it half-solved already? It should have, *but* it didn't.

Let me give you an example. Isabella and her partner, Benjamin, were in a slightly heated discussion. She was calmly and rationally trying to explain that she always felt small whenever Benjamin held grudges over small issues, ultimately causing problems where there weren't any. Benjamin once held a grudge for two days because she arrived at their dinner date late. And even if she had a completely understandable and reasonable excuse, he latched onto her lateness, thinking about it over and over again until he came to the ridiculous conclusion that her arriving late meant that she just didn't care enough and was looking for ways to break it off with him.

After patiently listening to what Isabella had to say, Benjamin selfishly pointed out that he had been hurt before, and that if she was a good partner, she would understand him and accept him the way he was. So, at this point, Benjamin understood the negative effects his past relationships and experiences had had on him; he just wasn't very willing to work on those negative effects.

As I said earlier, it's not enough to just acknowledge that you have a problem with anxiety and overthinking. Don't get me wrong, it is very essential to do so—but you also have to acknowledge the fact that it could cause you to hurt your partner, whether willingly or not, *and* you have to be willing to work on yourself. After all, relationships are a two-way street. Neither of you is perfect, but you ought to strive to be the best version of yourself for you and your partner.

Overthinking and anxiety are not only painful but also exhausting for both partners.

Letting go of overthinking and anxiety in relationships is never easy, but it's well worth it. If you are tired of always overthinking things and imagining worst-case scenarios in your relationships, then this workbook is for you. Overthinking can cause you to develop a narcissistic and pessimistic mindset. You become a person others try to avoid, and you automatically think the worst not only of yourself but also of other people. Essentially, you become a "glass half-empty" person, and you can no longer find happiness and satisfaction in your daily life and relationships. In your relationship as a couple, you find yourself lashing out at your partner, and you can't seem to stop hurting them. You might eventually become a full-blown bitter person with few or no loved ones around.

Is this what you want for yourself? Absolutely not, right? Then this relationship workbook is for you. In it, I have garnered my experiences with anxiety and overthinking. I struggled with anxiety and overthinking as a child, and in my relationships as an adult, I struggled with relationship anxiety. Realizing the problem I had was the first step; working on myself to become better (and yet making mistakes along the way) was the second.

I eventually started reading books about anxiety and overthinking, carrying out exercises to help me, talking to people who had similar experiences, and most importantly, I talked to my partner. I allowed myself to become vulnerable and I showed her every part of me, even the worst parts that scared me into thinking she might leave me. We also worked on trust and learning to communicate effectively with each other, not just yelling and not listening to ourselves. It wasn't easy; she also had to learn to be patient with me and to forgive me for the times I had hurt her with actions that stemmed from my overthinking and anxiety. Cut to now: we're married and have enjoyed many years together. We've surely had our ups and downs, but by the grace of God, with what we learned while we were still in courtship, and even what we learned inside marriage, we've had a truly beautiful marriage.

We have also been able to help a few of our friends who also had problems with their relationships due to anxiety and overthinking. Ben and Suzanne were one such couple. Ben was one of my closest friends, and Suzanne, my wife's. We always spent time together at least once a month on a double date. They were over for dinner one Sunday night and my wife and I couldn't help but notice that there seemed to be tension between them. At first, we thought it was probably just a little misunderstanding going on—until we all went out the next month on a double date and the tension between them had become so much worse. They were openly snapping and taking digs at each other. It went on like that until I had to ask, "Is everything all right between you two? You've been at each other's throats all night."

Suzanne, who seemed to have been waiting for that question, immediately launched into her side of the story. They eventually came home with us and we spent the entire night discussing what must have gone wrong between them. After praying and discussing what to do, my wife and I sat them down the following morning and we had another in-depth conversation, this time about the relationship anxiety that seemed to be plaguing them both and causing a strain on their marriage. We encouraged them to be open and honest with each other, teaching them the same tips and exercises that helped us. We also encouraged them not to feel ashamed or reluctant to see a Christian marriage counselor, if necessary.

The following weeks were fraught for them and also for us, but were well worth it in the end. They both grew in love for and understanding of each other.

It might be a long and difficult process, but I can assure you that reading this book will be of great help to you, your partner, and your relationship. In this book, you'll learn:

- The overthinking and anxiety cycle
- How overthinking and anxiety impact one's life
- What relationship anxiety looks like
- Possible causes of relationship anxiety
- The negative impact of anxiety on your relationship
- Brain exercises to rewire your anxious brain
- Working on trust and intimacy issues
- Creating healthy relationship habits
- The benefits of decluttering
- Mind and space decluttering
- Healthy coping habits for the overthinker
- And a whole lot more!

Are you ready to finally have that beautiful and anxiety-free relationship you've always wanted? Then let's dive in! I hope you enjoy the book.

PART ONE

Understanding Relationship Anxiety

In this part, you'll be obtaining an in-depth understanding of:

- The anxiety and overthinking cycle

- The possible causes of anxiety and overthinking

- The impact of anxiety and overthinking on your relationship

And in doing so, you'll not only begin to understand relationship anxiety, but you'll also be able to recognize the signs of relationship anxiety in yourself and/or your partner, as well as identify and understand the negative impact anxiety and overthinking has had (and/or is having) on your life and your relationship.

This will serve as a guide in taking that critical first step in rewiring your anxious brain and repairing the damage anxiety and overthinking might have had on you, your partner, and your relationship.

CHAPTER ONE

The Anxiety and Overthinking Cycle

"Anxiety in the heart of man causes depression, But a good word makes it glad."

—**Proverbs 12:25**

Laura found herself trapped in a never-ending cycle of anxiety and overthinking. Her thoughts seemed to have a life of their own, always dissecting scenarios and scrutinizing every little nuance of her conversations. She would analyze texts, look for underlying meanings, and repeat conversations in her brain, questioning every word she spoke. Her relationship with Mark started to suffer as a result of her incessant mental chatter, which always left her worn out and on edge.

You might think that you know what anxiety is: that person who always has sweaty palms, never makes eye contact, and just can't seem to be able to face a crowd—right? Actually, that's not quite it.

"Anxiety is your body's natural response to stress. It's a feeling of fear or apprehension about what's to come" (Holland, 2022). According to the American Psychological Association (the

APA), "Anxiety is an emotion characterized by feelings of tension, worried thoughts, and physical changes like increased blood pressure" (n.d.).

At one point or another, everyone has experienced anxiety. For example, you may worry and feel anxious if you have an important presentation to make, before taking an exam, or before making a life-changing decision. When this happens occasionally, it's quite normal and happens to the best of us. However, when it occurs too frequently, prevents you from living a normal life, and causes you to avoid situations (like missing school or faking an illness so you don't have to give a speech at your friend's wedding), then it could be that you have an anxiety disorder.

If your anxiousness feels overwhelming and is excessive and persistent, and it's not a reaction to a specific situation (like an exam or a presentation), then your anxiety symptoms may be "chronic and can interrupt [your] daily life" (Lindberg, 2021). According to the Anxiety & Depression Association of America, anxiety disorders are the most common mental health condition in the United States. The APA notes that anxiety disorders are not just the typical nerves you might feel from time to time; the anxiety is excessive and disruptive. Anxiety disorders affect nearly 30% of adults at some point in their lives.

Anxiety disorders include:

- Obsessive-compulsive disorder (OCD)

- Agoraphobia

- Post-traumatic stress disorder (PTSD)

- Social anxiety disorder

- Generalized anxiety disorder (GAD)

- Phobias

- Separation anxiety disorder

- Panic disorder

These will be discussed in more detail later on.

What is overthinking? Well, it "involves thinking about a certain topic or situation excessively and analyzing it for long periods of time" (Morin, 2023). It simply means you are unable to turn off your mind. It's like having a committee meeting going on all the time in your head. This happens when your mind spins and you make multiple U-turns and detours without reaching your intended destination.

Imagine this scenario: As you get comfortable in bed and try to fall asleep, your mind is full of ideas. You begin to overanalyze the conversations you had during the day, obsessing over what you said and didn't say. You imagine wildly different scenarios of how tomorrow's meeting might go, and you suddenly start wondering what the meaning of life is. You have officially entered the overthinking zone. And while it might originally seem harmless, overthinking eventually leads to a lot of problems and difficulties, ranging from the physical to the emotional.

Anxiety and Overthinking: Are They Intertwined?

Anxiety and overthinking. Like two peas in a pod, they appear to complement one another. They are usually intertwined, and one cannot exist without the other. Overthinking frequently gets its start from anxiety, that well-known state of uneasiness and fear. Anxiety sounds like a persistent voice in our thoughts that constantly imagines the worst-case scenario and questions every choice we make. In the meantime, overthinking is the overeager sidekick that follows anxiety's cues and analyzes, dissects, and overanalyzes every aspect of our life.

"Anxiety makes us overthink everything in many different ways, and the result of this overthinking isn't helpful at all" (Peterson, 2015). There are several ways through which anxiety causes overthinking (the list below is inspired by Tanya Peterson, author of several books on reducing anxiety):

1. Obsessively overanalyzing every conversation you have. You can't help thinking through every conversation, doing so over and over again until you come to a wildly inappropriate and false conclusion regarding how the conversation went or what it was *truly* about.

2. Having false beliefs about yourself and imagining bad scenarios that could develop as a result of that false belief.

3. Unnecessarily imagining worst-case scenarios that could occur as a result of you carrying out the activity that causes your anxiety (e.g., facing a crowd to give a presentation).

4. Thinking "what if?" and letting your mind run wild with the bad things that could happen. *What if...* These two simple words have the power to set off a torrent of terrifying thoughts, throwing our imaginations into an uproar.

5. Anxiety trains our minds to recognize potential dangers in our surroundings. While hypervigilance can be of great value in moments of true danger, it can also lead to overthinking in normal situations. Our minds become hyper-focused on imagined threats, exaggerating them and causing unnecessary scrutiny and anxiety.

6. Anxiety often coexists with perfectionism and a fear of failure. We put immense pressure on ourselves to meet unrealistically high standards, scared of making mistakes or falling short. This fear of failure causes overthinking as we constantly examine every move we

make, striving for perfection and fearing the outcome of any mistake.

I once read somewhere that anxiety and the overthinking that comes with it were more useful for our ancestors than they could ever be for us in the modern world. Imagine a man in the forest trying to hunt deer. He is extremely focused on the deer stripping off the bark of a tree just a few feet away from him when he realizes that the bushes behind him are rustling. His mind immediately goes into overdrive, thinking several thoughts at once. He tries to plan the outcome of every scenario that could develop—if the rustling is an animal hiding in the bushes, if it is a small or large animal, prey or foe, if he ought to escape or not, if he should remain still or not, what he would do if the deer got away… and so many more thoughts. Quite understandable, however, as it is the world he lives in. However, I highly doubt a rustling bush would mean a tiger is hiding and getting ready to attack you on your way home.

Anxiety and overthinking go hand in hand and almost always do more harm than good. It is up to us to figure out how to overcome it without losing touch with reality.

Ruminating and Worrying: The Overthinking Branches

Overthinking is a trap—one that most of us seem to have fallen into many times. I know I have, too many times to count. It involves "repetitively dwell[ing] on the same thought or situation over and over to the point that it disrupts your life" (Witmer, 2023). I know we all must have experienced that decision we just couldn't seem to make that kept us up at night.

It's quite normal. Everyone has had difficulty with making a decision and thinking too much about a particular thing. However, it becomes overthinking when you can't get it out of your head and it begins to affect you negatively.

Globally recognized motivational speaker Tony Robbins points out, "So when does thinking become *overthinking*? It's when you can't seem to turn your concerns off. It's when you think so much, you become paralyzed—unable to actually make a decision or take any action" (2023). Overthinking is like a massive, sprawling tree with many branches, and the most prominent of these branches are ruminating and worrying. These intertwined aspects of overthinking can consume our minds, trapping us in cycles of repetitive thinking and constant worrying.

Rumination

You must have heard the phrase "ruminating on the past." That's exactly what rumination involves: obsessively and repeatedly thinking about events that have occurred in the past, particularly the negative ones. Rumination is defined as "engaging in a repetitive negative thought process that loops continuously in the mind without end or completion" (Scolan, 2021). It is repeated musing about past events, conversations, mistakes, etc. It's like continually pressing the rewind and play buttons on a mental movie to dissect each scene and analyze it from every angle. This tendency to overthink keeps us stuck in the past and unable to fully engage with the present. We find ourselves unable to let go of what has already happened and endlessly wondering what could have happened and what should have happened.

Worrying

Worry, on the other hand, draws our attention to the future and involves uncertainty. It's a branch of overthinking that takes us into a realm of uncertainty and conjures up countless scenarios of potential harm and negative consequences. Worry can become all-encompassing as we struggle to deal with "what might happen" and find solace in the unknown.

Rumination and worry come in many forms, but they have one thing in common: being unable to get out of the bondage of thinking too much. Both thrive on overanalysis, dwelling on the past or the future, and magnifying potential problems. This constant cycle of rumination and worry* can lead to increased stress and anxiety, and even affect your ability to make clear decisions.

*Need help discovering the full cycle of Overthinking? Scan this QR Code to get to download the BONUS and get 2 e-books + 2 audiobooks on this topic.

Different Types of Anxiety

"Phew! That was close…"

Anxiety, which negatively affects daily life for so many of us, manifests itself in a variety of ways and also affects people in distinctive ways. Anxiety has different aspects, each with its challenges and manners of manifestation.

Anxiety is a normal reaction to perceived dangers or pressures that serves as a protective mechanism to prepare us for impending harm. However, anxiety disorders develop when anxiety becomes excessive, invasive, and affects daily living. Several diverse forms of anxiety disorders occur within this broad spectrum, each with its own set of triggers, symptoms, and underlying causes.

By gaining a deeper understanding of the different types of anxiety, we can better recognize and address the challenges they present. From generalized anxiety disorder (GAD) with its pervasive worry, to panic disorder, characterized by sudden and intense panic attacks, and social anxiety disorder (SAD), which is accompanied by profound fear in social situations, each anxiety disorder offers its own set of experiences and complexities. Here are some of the common types of anxiety disorders:

1. Generalized anxiety disorder: This disorder involves "excessive, unrealistic worry and tension with little or no reason" (WebMD Editorial Contributors, 2023) about different elements of life, such as your job, health, relationships, and everyday circumstances. Individuals with GAD frequently struggle to regulate their anxiety, which can interfere with everyday functioning. There may be symptoms such as "restlessness, fatigue, difficulty concentrating, irritability, muscle tension, or sleep disturbances" (DeMartini et al., 2019). GAD often manifests gradually and can have a major influence on a person's quality of life.

2. Obsessive-compulsive disorder (OCD): A person with OCD has difficulty controlling their thoughts and often engage in repetitive behaviors (Lindberg, 2021). By definition, OCD involves obsessions (invasive and

unwelcome thoughts that cause harsh suffering) and compulsions (repetitive behavioral or mental acts that individuals feel forced to carry out to ease their anxiety or forestall a dreaded outcome). Contamination worries, safety concerns, and undesired violent or forbidden ideas are common obsessions. Excessive cleaning, checking, or repeating rituals are common manifestations of compulsions. OCD may negatively influence everyday functioning and such individuals often need specialist treatment, such as counseling and medication.

3.   Panic disorder: According to the American Psychiatric Association (2023), "the core symptom of panic disorder is recurrent panic attacks, an overwhelming combination of physical and psychological distress." It is characterized by repeated and unpredictable panic attacks, which are intense bouts of anxiety or distress followed by physical symptoms such as heart palpitations, sweating, shaking, shortness of breath, chest pain, and a sense of impending doom. Panic attacks can occur without an obvious reason, leading to fear of future attacks and causing individuals to evade specific events or places to avoid a potential attack. Panic disorder can be extremely stressful, necessitating counseling and medication.

4. Phobia disorders: According to the National Institute of Mental Health (2023), a phobia is "an intense fear of—or aversion to—specific objects or situations." Phobia disorders are characterized by an excessive and illogical fear of certain items, events, or activities. The fear is exaggerated and not proportional to the harm that could be caused by the feared stimuli. Specific phobias (fear of spiders, heights, or flying, for example), social phobia (fear of social settings and being humiliated or embarrassed), and agoraphobia (fear of staying in locations or circumstances from which escape may be difficult, such as elevators) are examples of common phobias. Phobias can cause the individual to avoid certain situations or objects unnecessarily in a manner that could disrupt daily life.

5. Social anxiety disorder (SAD): This is "a fear or anxiety about social situations where you are exposed to judgement, scrutiny, or rejection in a social or performance situation" (Anthony, 2021). People with social anxiety often worry about embarrassing themselves or being humiliated, causing them to avoid social interactions, public speaking, or other performance situations. Physical symptoms like blushing, sweating, trembling, and rapid heartbeat are usually observed in social anxiety. Treatment options

include therapy, medication, and techniques like cognitive restructuring and social skills training.

6. Separation anxiety: Separation anxiety means feeling "very anxious or fearful when a person you're close to leaves your sight" (WebMD Editorial Contributors, 2023). It is usually found in children but can also affect adults. It involves extreme fear or anxiety about separation from attachment figures or from familiar environments. Children with separation anxiety may have difficulty attending school or being away from their parents, while adults may go through distress when separated from their significant other or home. Physical symptoms such as headaches, stomachaches, and nightmares can occur. Treatment for separation anxiety commonly involves therapy and gradually increasing exposure to separation situations.

7. Post-traumatic stress disorder (PTSD): According to the National Health Service (2023), PTSD is "an anxiety disorder caused by very stressful, frightening or distressing events." The symptoms of PTSD include intrusive thoughts about or flashbacks to the trauma, as well as nightmares, dissociation (feeling detached from reality), and feelings of sadness or guilt (Lok et al., 2018).

It is important to note that these anxiety disorders can coexist or present in different combinations. Each disorder has specific diagnostic criteria, treatment approaches, and potential causes, so you need to see a professional in order to be accurately diagnosed and treated.

The Vicious Anxiety Cycle

In medical biochemistry, there's something called the positive feedback system. In this system, the presence of a product leads to an increase in the activity of the system/pathway that led to the production of that product. Simply put, the more the presence and concentration of a certain chemical in the body, the more the body produces it… until it reaches a certain peak or crescendo, after which there is a decrease in the production of that chemical.

Take the anxiety cycle to be a positive feedback system, only a vicious one (don't let the word "positive" confuse you here!). When an event occurs that leads to you having symptoms of anxiety, you try to avoid the anxiety. This brings temporary relief—which doesn't last for long. Then the symptoms come back with a vengeance. And so, the more you try to avoid your anxiety, the stronger it gets.

Jaclyn Gulotta, PhD, LMHC, a licensed psychologist in Florida, explains, "The cycle of anxiety is when an event or situation happens and the person feels a lack of control or fear and avoids coping in order to escape intense emotions" (quoted in Mandriota, 2022).

This vicious cycle has four stages:

Stage 1: Anxiety and a desire to cope with it

Stage 2: Avoidance – trying to get out of the situation

Stage 3: Temporary relief

Stage 4: Heightened anxiety

Let's consider an example of the vicious anxiety cycle in a scenario involving a fear of flying:

Stage 1. Feeling anxious and wanting to deal with it:

Johnny has a fear of flying and has a business trip coming up that requires him to take a flight. As the travel date approaches, he starts feeling anxious about the upcoming flight and wants to find a way to cope with his fear.

Stage 2. Attempting to avoid the situation:

Johnny begins considering alternative modes of transportation to avoid flying. He explores options like driving or taking a train, believing that by avoiding air travel, he can prevent the anxiety and fear associated with flying.

Stage 3. Feeling a temporary sense of relief:

Once Johnny decides to drive instead of flying, he experiences a temporary sense of relief. He no longer has to face the fear-inducing situation of being on an airplane, and his anxiety subsides temporarily. This relief reinforces his belief that avoiding flying is an effective strategy for managing his fear.

Stage 4. Returning to a state of heightened anxiety:

As Johnny embarks on his road trip, he realizes that driving takes significantly longer and is more tiring than flying. He also becomes aware that his fear of flying has limited his ability to explore new destinations quickly and efficiently. These realizations trigger a return to a heightened state of anxiety as he worries about missing out on opportunities, facing long travel times, and not being able to fully participate in work-related activities.

Johnny's heightened anxiety may continue to reinforce his fear of flying and perpetuate the vicious anxiety cycle.

Brutal, isn't it? That's what anxiety does. The cycle eventually becomes deeply ingrained, making it harder to break free from its grip.

Signs You're an Overthinker

Overthinking is a common problem that affects some of us more than others. It entails incessantly overanalyzing circumstances, decisions, and discussions, which frequently leads to tension, worry, and indecision. If you find yourself engaged in an overthinking loop, here are some symptoms that you may be a chronic overthinker:

1. Difficulty making decisions: Overthinkers tend to struggle to make decisions, regardless of how big or small they might be. They overanalyze every possible outcome, weigh the pros and cons excessively, and dread making the wrong choice. This indecisiveness can lead to prolonged delays in taking action or even might even lead to avoiding decisions altogether.

2. Constant analysis and second-guessing: Overthinkers have a tendency to dissect past events and conversations, endlessly scrutinizing every detail and unnecessarily looking for hidden meanings. They always question themselves, replaying scenarios and imagining other outcomes that could have occurred, often leading to self-doubt and confusion.

3. Perfectionism: Overthinkers set high standards for themselves and expect everything to be flawless. They strive for perfection in their work, relationships, and personal life, which can lead to an excessive focus on details and an inability to accept imperfections or mistakes. This pursuit of perfection can be overwhelming and lead to a constant fear of failure.

4. Catastrophizing: Overthinkers have a tendency to catastrophize events, imagining the worst-case scenario. They are too concerned with things that have not yet occurred (and may never occur), causing unneeded stress and anxiety. This negative way of thinking can be

taxing and prevent individuals from appreciating the present moment.

5. Analysis paralysis: Overthinkers frequently become locked in a loop of analysis paralysis, in which they are so overwhelmed by the possibilities that they struggle to take any action at all. This can emerge in a variety of aspects of life, including job, relationships, and even routine daily tasks, resulting in missed opportunities and a sense of being trapped.

6. Seeking external approval: Before making judgments or taking action, overthinkers frequently seek reassurance and approval from others.

The Negative Effects on Your Life

Believe it or not, studies have shown that overthinking can actually impact your general sense of wellbeing (Toshi, 2023). The damaging effects of overthinking include, but are not limited to:

1. Damage to mental health: Constant overanalyzing creates a vicious cycle of mental harm (Chukuemeka, 2022). Overthinking drains you mentally, leaving you feeling listless and directionless after expending all your energy on thinking about your anxieties and worries (Nwokolo, 2022).

2. Impaired decision-making: Overthinking impairs your ability to make well-informed judgments. It's easy to get caught in the trap of indecision if you overanalyze every choice and dwell on potential consequences and alternative outcomes. As the fear of making the wrong choice increases, you'll waste great opportunities and come to dread making decisions. As a result, you may feel trapped and unable to progress in numerous aspects of your life.

3. Strain on relationships: Overthinking may have a bad influence on your relationships, which is probably why you are currently holding this book in your hands. Questioning your own behavior or the motives of others all the time can lead to misunderstandings, miscommunication, and avoidable fights. Overthinkers often interpret events incorrectly. Distance, mistrust, and tension can result in damaged personal and professional relationships.

4. Reduced creativity and innovation: Overthinking stifles creativity and innovation. When you are trapped in a cycle of overanalysis and self-doubt, it becomes difficult to think outside the box or take risks. Overthinkers tend to be overly cautious, fearing failure or criticism, which inhibits their ability to explore new ideas and approaches. This can hinder personal and professional growth, limiting your potential for success.

5. Sleep disturbances: Overthinking often causes disruptions to sleep patterns due to difficulty falling or staying asleep. The racing thoughts and worry can keep your mind active, making it difficult to get quality sleep. Lack of proper rest and sleep can also cause fatigue, irritability, and decreased cognitive functioning during the day.

Understanding Relationship Anxiety

"Relationship anxiety is when a person experiences persistent doubt, fear, or worry in a relationship" (Caporuscio, 2020). It is a common phenomenon in romantic partnerships. You may experience relationship anxiety due to "attachment difficulties in early childhood, emotional neglect, or from general anxiety that manifests as worry in your relationships" (Powell, 2022).

The most common causes include, but are not limited to:

- Low self-esteem

- Toxic past relationships

- Trauma

- Environmental factors

- Traditional and cultural norms

These will be discussed in detail later on.

Signs Your Relationship Anxiety Has Become Unhealthy

Here are some indicators that you need to get a handle on your relationship anxiety and perhaps seek professional help:

1. Constant worrying: Persistent and intrusive thoughts about the relationship or excessive worry about your partner's feelings, commitment, or potential problems, even when there is no concrete evidence to support your concerns, can be problematic.

2. Fear of rejection or abandonment: Relationship anxiety can manifest as a deep-seated fear of being rejected or abandoned by your partner. This fear may lead to clingy behavior, possessiveness, or an overwhelming need for reassurance and validation.

3. Overanalyzing and doubting: As someone experiencing relationship anxiety, you may tend to overanalyze every aspect of the relationship. You question your partner's intentions, doubt the authenticity of their love, or search for hidden meanings behind their words and actions. This constant doubt can strain the relationship and create unnecessary tension.

4. Avoidance and withdrawal: Relationship anxiety leads to a tendency to avoid or withdraw from the relationship. Scared of possible rejection or abandonment, you may create emotional distance, avoid difficult conversations, or even contemplate

ending the relationship as a way of protecting yourself from perceived harm.

5. Neglecting self-care: When relationship anxiety becomes overwhelming, you may neglect self-care and prioritize the relationship above your own wellbeing. You may excessively focus on the needs and wants of your partner, sacrificing your own interests, friendships, and personal growth. This imbalance can lead to feelings of resentment and dissatisfaction, further exacerbating the relationship anxiety.

If you notice these signs in yourself or your relationship, it is important to accept them for what they are (no denial) and seek support. Remember, addressing and working through relationship anxiety can lead to personal growth, improved wellbeing, and a stronger, more fulfilling relationship.

MAIN IDEAS

Remember Laura?

One day, Laura decided that enough was enough. She recognized that her anxiety and overthinking were holding her back from truly enjoying life and maintaining a healthy relationship. She started to read and learn about anxiety and overthinking, especially relationship anxiety. She looked back at her past relationships and decided to forgive those who had hurt her. She prayed, too; she talked to God about everything and held on to all the Bible had to say on anxiety. With determination and the support of therapy, she started implementing strategies to quiet her racing mind. Gradually, she learned to challenge her negative thoughts, practice mindfulness, and engage in self-care activities. As she gained control over her anxious tendencies, Laura felt a newfound sense of freedom and a deeper connection with Mark. The cycle was finally broken, and she embraced a life filled with peace, confidence, and a brighter outlook on the future.

Anxiety and overthinking frequently coexist, forming a complicated and interwoven cycle that can be difficult to break. Overthinking is a symptom of anxiety in which excessive worry and rumination take center stage. This persistent cycle of overthinking feeds worry, creating a feedback loop that worsens both mental states. We tend to overthink more when we are nervous or stressed. Overthinking has many branches, including ruminating and worrying. Ruminating is repeated attention on negative ideas, events, or memories, whereas worrying is excessive anticipation of prospective negative results. These two characteristics of overthinking can waste a large amount of mental energy and contribute to anxiety's persistence.

Understanding the many types of anxiety, identifying the indications of overthinking, and realizing the detrimental effects on one's life are all important stages in breaking free from this cycle.

Relationship anxiety can add another layer of complication. It is characterized by excessive anxiety and uncertainty about one's romantic connection, which frequently leads to insecurity, mistrust, and emotional pain. Recognizing indicators of unhealthy relationship anxiety, such as continual doubt, lack of trust, or difficulty maintaining a healthy emotional connection, is critical for obtaining help and treating these issues before they have a negative influence on one's wellbeing and relationships.

WORKBOOK ONE

Exercise 1: Self-Assessment

Take a moment to reflect on your relationship anxiety and answer the following questions:

- Do you frequently doubt the stability and future of your romantic relationship?

- Are you constantly seeking reassurance from your partner about their feelings for you?

- Do you often experience intense jealousy or possessiveness in your relationship?

- Are you overly sensitive to perceived signs of rejection or abandonment?

- Do you find yourself constantly questioning your partner's actions and motives?

Suggested Practice: Relationship Anxiety Self-Reflection

Take some time to journal about your relationship anxiety using the following prompts:

- Reflect on specific instances when you have experienced anxiety or worry in your relationship. What were the triggers for these feelings?

- How does your relationship anxiety impact your emotional wellbeing and overall relationship satisfaction?

- Consider any patterns or recurring thoughts that contribute to your relationship anxiety. Are there any underlying fears or insecurities driving these thoughts?

- Explore the ways in which your relationship anxiety affects your behavior and interactions with your partner. How does it influence your communication, trust, and ability to be vulnerable?

- Think about any previous experiences or past relationships that may be contributing to your relationship anxiety. How have these experiences shaped your current mindset?

Suggested Practice: Relationship Anxiety Awareness

Pay attention to your relationship anxiety in your day-to-day interactions with your partner. Take note of the following:

- Identify triggers: What situations, behaviors, or thoughts tend to trigger your relationship anxiety?

- Notice your physical sensations: How does your body react when you experience relationship anxiety? Are there any specific physical symptoms, such as increased heart rate or muscle tension?

- Observe your thought patterns: What kind of thoughts run through your mind during moments of relationship anxiety? Are they realistic or based on assumptions and fears?

- Monitor your behavior: How does your relationship anxiety influence your actions and reactions towards your partner? Are there any patterns of avoidance, clinginess, or seeking excessive reassurance?

- Reflect on the impact: Consider how your relationship anxiety affects both you and your partner. Does it create distance, tension, or strain in the relationship?

Remember, self-assessment and self-reflection are essential steps in understanding and addressing relationship anxiety. These exercises and practices will help you gain insights into your specific anxieties and lay the groundwork for developing healthier coping mechanisms and strategies in your relationship.

CHAPTER TWO

Exploring the Causes

"Have I not commanded you? Be strong and of good courage; do not be afraid, nor be dismayed, for the Lord your God is with you wherever you go."

—Joshua 1:9

"Healing doesn't mean the damage never existed, it means the damage no longer controls our lives."

—**Anonymous**

As Raven sat on her porch swing, sipping her morning tea, her mind wandered back to the early days of her relationship with James. They'd been inseparable, always laughing and sharing their dreams. But as time passed, a veil of anxiety and overthinking seemed to settle over their once blissful connection. Raven often found herself questioning James' love and commitment, dissecting every word and action for hidden meanings. The fear of being hurt or abandoned consumed her, leaving her in a constant state of unease.

Reflecting on their journey, Raven realized that the causes of her anxiety and overthinking were rooted in past experiences. She had been hurt before, betrayed by someone she thought she could trust. Those wounds had never fully healed, and they cast a shadow over her current relationship. Raven understood that her overanalyzing was a defense mechanism, an attempt to protect herself from potential heartbreak. It wasn't James' actions that fueled her anxiety, but rather her own fears and insecurities that needed addressing.

Relationship anxiety, no doubt, places massive strain on a relationship. So much so that it can eventually cause the relationship to become toxic and emotionally draining for both partners, regardless of which partner is suffering from relationship anxiety. One of the ways by which you can understand and overcome it is to understand the underlying cause of it. Knowing and understanding the reason why you or your partner has relationship anxiety brings you much closer to overcoming it and achieving a much healthier mindset in and towards your relationship.

In this chapter, we'll be talking about possible causes of relationship anxiety in detail, so let's get right to it.

Your Past Relationships Matter

"Relationship problems occur when expectations from past relationships are applied to the current participants in a new relationship" (Woods, 2021). Your past relationships and the experiences you have had in those relationships can play a major role in shaping your future relationship(s).

Think about it: why do people who have experienced what it's like to be cheated on find it difficult to trust their new partner? Why do people who were emotionally manipulated become cold and seemingly unfeeling? Their past relationship has caused them to, in the first example, become unable to trust others, and in the second instance, develop a self-protective measure that prevents them from having true intimacy with their partners.

Exploring the causes of relationship anxiety in terms of previous relationships provides a more in-depth understanding of how past experiences influence your current mindset and behavior.

1. Trust issues: Betrayal, infidelity, or broken trust in previous relationships can cause deep-seated trust issues. The mental and sometimes physical scars left by such experiences can make it truly difficult to trust and fully open yourself in future relationships. Relationship anxiety might then develop as a protective strategy against future hurt and disappointment.

2. Abuse: Being in an abusive or toxic relationship can have a significant effect on your trust, self-esteem, and general wellbeing. Abuse, whether emotional, physical, or psychological, can cause long-term tension and anxiety in later relationships. Scars from previous

violent relationships may cause hypervigilance, dread of experiencing the same thing, and anxiety.

3. Patterns and repetition: Patterns in relationships are common, especially when unresolved issues from the past go untreated. If you find yourself repeating the same relationship dynamics or attracting people who demonstrate similar bad habits, it might worsen your relationship anxiety. Recognizing and addressing these behaviors is critical for breaking the cycle and cultivating healthy relationships.

Low Self-Esteem

Your self-esteem is basically "your opinion of yourself" (Whelan, 2022). If you have low self-esteem, it "essentially means having a poor opinion of yourself" (Cherry, 2023). Individuals with low self-esteem frequently doubt their own value and believe they are insufficient, unlovable, or undeserving of love and pleasure. These poor self-perceptions can have a significant impact on our relationships and contribute to anxiety and overthinking in a variety of ways, including:

1. Constant need for validation: Low self-esteem can lead to a constant need for external validation from your partner. People with low self-esteem often rely heavily on their partner's approval to feel safe and worthy. They seek repeated affirmation of love and acceptance. This

excessive need for approval can strain the relationship as the other partner begins to feel overwhelmed or unable to satisfy the insatiable need for approval.

2. Negative self-talk and overthinking: People with low self-esteem often have negative inner monologues and constant self-criticism. You may brood over past failures, ruminate on your shortcomings, and constantly fear that you are not good enough. This can lead to overanalyzing every interaction, conversation, and decision as you constantly question your partner's feelings, intentions, and loyalty.

3. Jealousy and insecurity: Low self-esteem frequently fuels feelings of jealousy and insecurity in relationships. Individuals who feel intimidated by perceived competition may continuously compare themselves to others. They may assume that their partner will eventually find someone more suitable and deserving of their affection. Jealousy and insecurity can rise to the level of possessiveness and a constant need for reassurance, straining the relationship even further.

Overcoming low self-esteem and minimizing relationship anxiety and overthinking necessitates self-reflection, self-compassion, and active self-esteem-building efforts.

"Why is he with me?" "I can't believe someone like her is with someone like me." Thoughts like this not only destroy you as a person, but can place unnecessary pressure on your partner and strain your relationship. Besides, what do you think is so wrong with you? What does the Bible say about you? What does God say about you? Do you see yourself that way?

"Because you are precious in my eyes and honored, and I love you, I give men in return for you, people in exchange for your life."—Isaiah 43:4

"For you created my innermost being; you knit me together in my mother's womb. I praise you because I am fearfully and wonderfully made; your works are wonderful, I know that full well."—Psalm 139:13–14

The Role of Trauma

This may seem to be quite similar to the first point in this chapter (your past relationships matter). However, traumatic experiences are not limited to past relationships. Trauma can occur as a result of any intensely stressful event or situation (Leonard, 2020). "Traumatic events can happen at any age and have lasting effects on your physical and mental well-being" (Ryder, 2022). In turn, this will likely affect your capacity to create and sustain good relationships.

Traumatic experiences can lead to post-traumatic stress disorder, which we discussed in the previous chapter. As a quick reminder, PTSD is "a psychiatric disorder characterized by intrusive thoughts, nightmares, flashbacks, and hyperarousal" (American Psychiatric Association, 2013). Individuals with PTSD often experience anxiety and overthinking related to their traumatic experiences, which can significantly affect their relationships (Cloitre et al., 2009).

Trauma can erode an individual's ability to trust others, especially their romantic partners. Past experiences of betrayal, abuse, or abandonment can lead to anxiety and overthinking, making it challenging to establish and maintain healthy intimacy in relationships (Feiring & Taska, 2005). Trauma can also significantly impact an individual's self-esteem and self-worth. Those who have experienced trauma may develop negative beliefs about themselves and struggle with feelings of worthlessness and inadequacy.

These feelings can, in turn, contribute to relationship anxiety and overthinking (Szymanski & Kashubeck-West, 2014). As a result, trauma survivors may use coping methods such as avoidance and emotional detachment as a form of self-protection. These strategies can hinder their ability to engage fully in relationships, leading to anxiety and overthinking (Katz & Windecker-Nelson, 2004).

Understanding the impact of trauma on relationship dynamics is critical for creating a successful therapeutic approach and support networks for those who have been traumatized.

Your Attachment Style Also Matters

Everyone has an attachment style, but not many people are aware that this is a thing (Izuakam, 2023). Your attachment style refers to how you behave in your relationships with others (Gonsalves, 2023). Attachment "is the emotional connection you formed as an infant with your primary caregiver—probably your mother" (Robinson et al., 2023). In the field of psychology, attachment theory "proposes that each and every one of us has an attachment style that developed when we were very young" (McDermott, 2023). As Robinson et al. (2023) explain, "According to attachment theory, pioneered by British psychiatrist John Bowlby and American psychologist Mary Ainsworth, the quality of the bonding you experienced during this first relationship often determines how well you relate to other people and respond to intimacy throughout life."

Basically, your attachment style comes from your experiences during childhood and plays a crucial role in shaping how you and maintain relationships. It can also impact whether or not you have relationship anxiety (Bowlby, 1969). Attachment theory suggests that early experiences with caregivers shape individuals' expectations and beliefs about relationships throughout their lives (Bowlby, 1969).

The theory identifies three primary attachment styles: secure, anxious (or preoccupied), and avoidant.

Secure Attachment Style

Securely attached individuals view themselves and other people positively (Mikulincer & Shaver, 2016). They typically had consistent and responsive caregiving during their early childhood, which helped them develop a sense of security and confidence in relationships. In romantic relationships, they are less likely to engage in excessive worrying, jealousy, or possessiveness (Simpson et al., 2007). They have a positive self-image and trust in their partners, which contributes to a sense of security and reduces the need for constant reassurance or validation. Their secure base in childhood serves as a model for secure relationships in adulthood, creating a cycle of healthy attachment patterns.

In summary, secure attachment style is characterized by a positive view of oneself and others, trust, and comfort with intimacy. Individuals with a secure attachment style experience lower levels of relationship anxiety and overthinking, leading to greater relationship satisfaction and stability.

Anxious Attachment Style

Anxious attachment style involves fear of abandonment and a simultaneous need to be close to others, as well as anxiety about relationships in general (Mikulincer & Shaver, 2016). Individuals with an anxious attachment style frequently have a history of unpredictable, inconsistent caregiving in their early years, which leads to feelings of insecurity and a constant need for reassurance and validation in their relationships. This leads them to overthink and overanalyze their partner's behaviors (Ein-Dor et al., 2015).

Research shows that anxiously attached individuals are more likely to experience relationship anxiety (Cassidy & Shaver, 2016) because of their tendency to view normal behavior as an indication of rejection on the part of their partner. This leads to reassurance-seeking behaviors in the anxiously attached person (Ein-Dor et al., 2015). The accompanying negative thought patterns and anxious behaviors contribute to a cycle of anxiety and overthinking, which can undermine relationship satisfaction and stability.

In summary, those with an anxious attachment style have a heightened need for reassurance and tend to engage in overthinking. Their fear of rejection and abandonment can lead to maladaptive thoughts and behaviors in romantic relationships.

Avoidant Attachment Style

Those with an avoidant attachment style tend to be emotionally distant from their romantic partner, as in childhood they typically experienced unresponsive or inconsistent care from their parents or caregivers (Mikulincer & Shaver, 2016). Individuals with an avoidant attachment style value self-reliance, self-sufficiency, and autonomy, which might affect their behavior and interactions in romantic relationships.

As a result, these individuals develop a coping mechanism: suppressing their own needs and emotions (Bartholomew & Horowitz, 1991). They can use this coping mechanism to reduce the perceived hazards of emotional reliance and vulnerability. As a result, they frequently avoid seeking intimacy, rely only on themselves for support, and keep an emotional distance from their partner. They may also dismiss or suppress how they feel (Feeney & Noller, 1990). These shields act as a safeguard against potential rejection or disappointment. However, these protective systems can exacerbate marital problems by impeding open and honest communication and preventing the building of trust.

In summary, individuals with an avoidant attachment style tend to prioritize independence and self-reliance in relationships. They may exhibit emotional distancing, avoidance of intimacy, and suppression of attachment-related needs and emotions.

Understanding attachment styles and promoting secure attachment can contribute to healthier and more fulfilling relationships.

The Connection Between Physical Health and Emotional Wellbeing

"Hey, nice to meet you! You don't mind if I bring this with me, right?"

Have you ever experienced something like this: you're sleep-deprived or haven't had a proper meal all day, and you find yourself snapping at people or being a grumpy bear in general. Well, this happens to almost everyone. However, intense strain on one's physical health can also cause strain on one's relationship and possibly eventually damage the relationship.

If we're physically ill, it significantly increases our risk of becoming mentally ill as well (and vice versa). According to the Mental Health Foundation (2022), "Nearly one in three people with a long-term physical health condition also has a mental health problem, most often depression or anxiety."

The Effect of Environmental Factors

"The environment and mental health are intrinsically connected. The places where you spend a lot of time—home, work, school, and even socially—can have a significant impact on your mental well-being" (Lindberg, 2023). Furthermore, "some aspects of environmental experience have long-term effects, through mechanisms that have not yet been identified, on levels of anxiety and depression symptoms" (Kendler et al., 2011).

In fact, our environment can even alter our brains—research has shown that "children raised in adverse environments tend to have hindered brain development, increasing their risk of memory issues, learning difficulties, and behavioral problems" (Lindbergh, 2023). Just as the environment can affect our brains, it can also impact us psychologically, potentially affecting stress levels, and therefore our overall mental health (Helbich, 2018).

Also, think about this … Who are your friends? Who are the people you surround yourself with? What are they like? Think in particular about the ones whoa re currently in a relationship or married. How do they treat their significant others? When you go out, what do you notice them doing to their partners or vice versa? Are there any behaviors you normally wouldn't be comfortable with, but you've grown accustomed to and they don't faze you anymore, such as belittlement, disregard of feelings and opinions, or disrespectful behavior?

These acts are oftentimes not glaringly obvious. They are mostly subtle and might even seem like acts of love or normal behavior. You'll find that you may have begun to do the same to your partner, or perhaps you also accept such treatment regardless of how it makes you feel.

The Impact of Cultural and Societal Norms

Anxiety and overthinking in relationships can be influenced by cultural and societal norms, as these factors play a significant role in shaping individuals' beliefs, expectations, and behaviors within intimate partnerships. Cultural and societal norms encompass a range of factors, including gender roles, relationship ideals, communication patterns, and expectations regarding love and commitment. Understanding the impact of these norms can provide insights into the causes of your anxiety and overthinking.

Traditional gender roles often assign different responsibilities and expectations to each gender, which can create pressure and lead to relationship anxiety. For example, in many cultures, women are expected to prioritize caregiving and emotional support in relationships, while men are expected to be strong, independent, and provide financially (Christopher & Cate, 2018). These rigid gender roles can lead to feelings of inadequacy, anxiety about meeting societal expectations, and overthinking about one's performance in the relationship.

Cultural and societal norms that promote relationship ideals can also contribute to anxiety and overthinking. Movies, TV shows, and popular culture frequently depict idealized love relationships that may not always match reality. These idealized representations can lead to excessive expectations and put pressure on people to conform to the standards of a "perfect" relationship. Research has shown that exposure to such idealized relationships can create anxiety and dissatisfaction when real life does not meet these standards (Knobloch-Westerwick & Alter, 2017).

Anxiety and overthinking in relationships can also be influenced by the communication patterns dictated by societal conventions. In some cultures, indirect communication is valued, and people may be hesitant to voice their demands and problems directly. Meanwhile, those who dread confrontation or potential conflict may experience anxiety in cultures that value aggressively straightforward communication.

It is important to keep in mind that cultural and societal norms vary greatly across regions, and subgroups within countries. The effect of these norms on anxiety and overthinking in relationships will also differ. Furthermore, people may absorb and interpret norms differently, resulting in a range of experiences and responses within the same cultural setting.

Recognizing the impact of these societal standards can help us manage our relationships with more understanding and open discussions, resulting in happier and more fulfilling relationships.

Other Causes of Anxiety and Overthinking in Relationships

1. Lack of relationship role models: Growing up without healthy relationship role models or witnessing harmful relationship dynamics can have an impact on your attitudes and expectations about relationships. You may struggle to understand the boundaries of healthy relationships if you did not have positive models to learn from.

2. Fear of rejection or abandonment: Being rejected or abandoned can leave emotional wounds. These events can cause anxiety in relationships by instilling dread of being rejected or abandoned again. Fear of re-experiencing that hurt and humiliation might cause you to doubt your worthiness of love and generate a perpetual sense of unease.

MAIN IDEAS

Let's return to Raven for a moment. With her newfound awareness, Raven mustered the courage to have an open conversation with James. She bared her soul, sharing her struggles and the reasons behind her anxieties. To her relief,

James responded with empathy and understanding, assuring her of his unwavering love and commitment. He, too, had noticed the strain in their relationship and was willing to work together to overcome it.

Embracing vulnerability, Raven and James embarked on a journey of healing and growth. They attended couples therapy, seeking professional guidance in navigating their insecurities and building a stronger foundation. Through this process, they learned to communicate more openly, practicing active listening and offering reassurances when needed. As the days turned into weeks and the weeks into months, Raven's anxiety gradually loosened its grip on their relationship. Trust flourished, and their connection blossomed into a deeper, more resilient bond. Together, they transformed their shared love story into one of resilience, reminding each other that healing and growth are possible even in the face of past traumas.

The causes of anxiety and overthinking in relationships form an intricate web of psychological, relational, and societal influences. Past events, such as prior traumas or unfavorable interpersonal dynamics, might contribute to anxiety and overthinking on an individual level. These habits might also be fueled by insecurities, low self-esteem, and a fear of abandonment or rejection. External constraints and societal expectations, such as cultural norms or media influences, can also heighten concerns about the perceived "success" of the relationship or keeping up appearances. Understanding these factors enables us to identify the underlying causes of our anxiety and overthinking, allowing us to handle them more effectively and create healthier interpersonal dynamics.

Relationship dynamics, in addition to individual considerations, can play a substantial part in the development of anxiety and overthinking. Lack of trust, poor communication, or frequent confrontations can create an unpredictable environment and foster anxious thoughts. Unresolved concerns from the past, as well as ongoing habits of emotional neglect or inconsistency, can contribute to anxiety. Furthermore, unreasonable expectations, such as demanding perfection or frequent reassurance, can lead to overthinking and further strain on the relationship.

WORKBOOK TWO

Section 1: Personal Reflection

1. Reflect on your personal history. Are there any past experiences or traumas that may have contributed to your anxiety and overthinking in your relationships?

2. Consider your self-perception and self-esteem. How does your self-image impact your anxiety and overthinking patterns within relationships?

3. Explore any underlying fears or insecurities that may be triggering your anxieties. Are there specific fears of abandonment, rejection, or failure that contribute to your overthinking?

Section 2: Relationship Dynamics

4. Analyze your current or past relationship dynamics. Have there been instances of trust being broken or inconsistent behavior that have contributed to your anxiety and overthinking?

5. Reflect on the communication patterns within your relationships. Do misunderstandings or a lack of open communication contribute to your overthinking? How do conflicts affect your anxiety levels?

6. Consider the influence of external factors on your relationship. How do societal expectations, cultural

norms, or media portrayals impact your anxieties about relationship "success" or outward appearances?

Section 3: Patterns and Triggers

7. Identify recurring patterns in your anxious thoughts. Are there specific situations or triggers that consistently lead to anxiety and overthinking in your relationships?

8. Reflect on the role of control in your relationships. Do you feel a need to control outcomes or constantly seek reassurance? How does this contribute to your anxiety and overthinking?

9. Explore any perfectionistic tendencies or unrealistic expectations you may have for yourself or your partner. How do these expectations fuel anxiety and overthinking?

Conclusion:

Reflect on the insights gained from this workbook. Acknowledge the causes of your anxiety and overthinking in relationships, both personal and relational. It is a critical step in letting go of anxiety and overthinking in your relationships.

CHAPTER THREE

The Impact of Anxiety and Overthinking on Relationships

"Blessed is the man who trusts in the Lord, And whose hope is the Lord. For he shall be like a tree planted by the waters, Which spreads out its roots by the river, And will not fear when heat comes; But its leaf will be green, And will not be anxious in the year of drought, Nor will cease from yielding fruit."
—Jeremiah 17:7,8

"Anxiety is love's greatest killer. It makes others feel as you might when a drowning man holds on to you. You want to save him, ut you know he will strangle you with his panic."
—Anaïs Nin

The impact of worry and overthinking on relationships is best defined as "catastrophic." Daniel had been a worrywart for as long as anyone could remember. When he was a child, it was cute to have a responsible kid who never forgot to do the dishes or pick up his younger siblings from school, but as he grew older, it became clear that his overthinking was driving people away from him, and this realization came only after his breakup with Lauren.

Being a constant worrier indicates that your relaxation switch is faulty. This means the mind of an overthinker like Daniel is always in overdrive, and for him, it was almost impossible to get his mind off the little things. Once he fixated on something, there was no room for anything else, and this slowly drove a wedge between him and Lauren.

Being an overthinker can make your relationships a bit strenuous, but it is still possible to make meaningful connections and maintain a romantic relationship if you manage your anxiety properly.

Relationship Anxiety: More Than Just Jealousy and Insecurity

It's normal to feel jealous sometimes. Jealousy tends to occur "when someone feels insecure about their relationship" (Stritof, 2022). In the context of a romantic relationship, jealousy can come in the form of resentment, hatred, worry, or uncertainty that your partner may leave you or interact with others more successfully than you do. It is caused by a lack of self-assurance and a fear of losing someone. Everyone is wired to experience jealousy, but when it gets illogical, it can be toxic. Irrational, unhealthy jealousy stems from "fear of abandonment and a worry about not being truly loved" (Rodriguez et al., 2016) and frequently results in mistreatment of one's partner.

Unhealthy jealousy is generally caused by mistrust. Individuals with anxiety tend to have less trust in people, which makes them test their partners whenever they can, leading to obsessive thought patterns about their partners being unfaithful, which then gives rise to bitterness and develops into jealousy over time. Jealousy is an irrational fear of losing something or someone which is or who's yours already. Obsessive thinking spells doom for almost every relationship. Why? Because people who overthink tend to find faults in even the littlest of things, which leads to jealousy or insecurity. For people with anxiety, jealousy and insecurity are programmed right alongside their anxiety; their lack of trust gives rise to fear, which brings about jealousy.

At some point, "jealous people feel so overwhelmed by their emotions and insecurities that they begin to exert control over their partners" (Stritof, 2022). Some of the behaviors that might show up are:

- Going through one's partner's emails, texts and call logs
- Searching one's partner's personal belongings
- Interrogating one's partner at every opportunity
- Overreacting and getting mad over small or irrelevant issues

Unfortunately, jealousy typically ends up causing resentment and defensiveness on the part of the other partner (Rodriguez,

2015) and "wreaks havoc on a relationship as the jealous person becomes more and more fearful, angry, and controlling" (Stritof, 2022).

Common Negative Behaviors Associated with These Traits

We all feel anxious at times—it's a normal part of life—but keep in mind that "chronic anxiety can interfere with your quality of life" (Cherney, 2022). It shouldn't be surprising by now to learn that anxiety and overthinking have a harmful impact on the human mind and body. The repercussions can be physical or psychological, and, if left unchecked, have debilitating implications. Negative behaviors related to these attributes are more common than most people realize, including:

1. Insomnia or poor sleeping habits: I believe we barely value the ability to sleep at will; imagine not being able to sleep even when you are thoroughly exhausted. We all like to get some good shuteye, right? But for people struggling with anxiety, loss of sleep is pretty much normal, as they oftentimes have trouble sleeping due to overthinking. They are always lost in their thoughts, and the obsessive thought patterns make it hard for the body to relax enough to go into sleep mode.

2. Drug addiction: Constantly thinking about the same things is enough to drive someone nuts. Some people

cope in healthy ways, but for others, it's more difficult, and they turn to drugs to help them unwind and relax.

3. Poor time management and a drop in productivity: Being an overthinker, or worrywart as I like to call it, implies that a person will fixate on one thing for hours and shut out everything else, no matter how urgent their other tasks that day may be. The decline in productivity is due to difficulty keeping track of time as well as an inability to concentrate.

4. Mood swings: People who suffer from anxiety tend to be irritable and quick to become depressed. This is due to their uncertainty, fear, and repetitive thought processes, which makes them more volatile and prone to melancholy and negativity (Knight, 2023).

5. Restlessness and indecisiveness: This is possibly the most common habit in people who suffer from anxiety and overthinking. This is because they overanalyze everything, making it difficult to make decisions and preventing them "from recognizing the evidence needed for problem-solving and making rational decisions" (Knight, 2023).

6. High blood pressure, illness, and exhaustion: These are some of the physical consequences of overthinking and anxiety. Overthinking "has been linked to physical health issues such as anxiety, depression, obsessive-

compulsive disorder (OCD), post-traumatic stress disorder (PTSD), chronic fatigue, insomnia and sleep disruption" (Knight, 2023).

Anxiety Issues and Codependency

"I'm sure there was more than this yesterday."

Another word for having an anxious attachment style is being "codependent" (McLean, 2021). Codependency is a dysfunctional way to approach relationships—it involves one partner completely sacrificing their own needs and desires for the sake of the other. And codependency doesn't only exist in romantic relationships; it can be found between parent and child, friends, and family members just as easily.

While anxiety is defined as a feeling of uncertainty or dread, codependency in this context is an attachment or reliance on someone as a result of this anxiety.

There are two types of anxiety in relationships: isolation anxiety and relationship attachment anxiety. Individuals who suffer from isolation anxiety in relationships are withdrawn and prefer to be alone. They may be irritable and cranky. They are not inherently bad people; they simply prefer to be alone, and when they are in relationships, they expect (or rather demand) that their partners be helpful and accommodating, despite the fact that this is not how a healthy relationship should operate. People with this type of anxiety don't know how to make concessions and expect everyone else to bow and adhere to their will, which leads to the relationship becoming nearly dictatorial in nature—which no one wants.

Relationship attachment anxiety occurs when someone suffocates their partner due to anxiety or fear of abandonment. The worried person is constantly watching their partner; it's similar to jealousy without evidence of something to be jealous about. Individuals with this type of anxiety are drawn to isolated individuals, and this is where codependency begins.

Individuals with codependent traits seek the approval of others (most notably their partners) and bury their own needs and wants in an attempt to please their partners, and slowly, without either of them even realizing it, they begin to lose themselves. Some are so far gone that they cannot even distinguish their own desires from those of their partner. They are also often extremely clingy—and not the cute kind of clingy that makes you feel cherished, but one that frustrates their partners and makes them feel suffocated.

While it is obviously okay to express your affection for your partner, you must be careful not to suffocate them with your emotions. People with a tendency to be codependent spend a lot of time and resources attempting to help or "fix" their partner, and when they fail, their inner overthinker explodes and starts fretting over everything. While people may believe that the anxious/codependent individual's actions are unselfish, in reality they are not: everything they do is in an attempt to control their own anxiety. They internalize the fears, emotions, and difficulties of others, leaving them in a condition of continual anxiety and paranoia. They also find it difficult to express their feelings since they believe they are unimportant and come second to those of their partner.

Anxious people with codependent traits fear criticism and being perceived as not good enough, which is why they try their hardest to make their partner happy even at the expense of their own happiness. Certain past experiences, such as being criticized by their boss at work or being criticized by their parents as a child, can exacerbate the anxiety. These people are so focused on assisting their partner with everything that they end up feeling drained and overwhelmed, causing them to become unreasonable, irritable, and exhausted.

The Impact of Overthinking and Anxiety on Communication in Relationships

Communication is simply the exchange of opinions, ideas, and thoughts between parties—in this case, between romantic partners. Communication is the key to relationships, and it can be verbal or non-verbal, ranging from eye contact to direct conversation. Most couples, after years of being together, are able to convey information through mere gestures or expressions.

One couple I can think of, for example, were always traveling separately around the world on business, but after retirement, they discovered they had spent decades texting and video calling, which made it difficult for them to express themselves face to face. They realized they weren't good at it and went on communicating by phone. Even though they live in the same house, they spend more time calling each other and having text conversations than talking in person. Others may find it strange, but this is exactly what works for them.

Communication can make or break a relationship; without communication, you and your partner cannot talk and express your feelings. Constant, open communication builds lasting relationships, and talking about both the little things and the big things brings you closer together.

Lack of communication, on the other hand, will break the relationship. It starts slowly for most, as you start to grow distant from each other, question each other, and assume the worst when the solution to the problem might simply be to talk it out. Yes, talking it out is a way of finding solutions to arguments and everyday problems in a relationship. Lack of communication, therefore, is like a parasite which slowly eats at the relationship until it becomes a shell or husk of its former self.

A relationship is like a computer and anxiety is a computer virus, and communication is the firewall preventing the loss of files (which in this situation is the relationship). This means the more you and your partner communicate with each other, the lesser the chances of the two of you growing apart. An overthinker * or worrywart is not able to express their feelings to their other half because they find it hard to have conversations without obsessing over the little things that oftentimes don't even matter, and because of that they dread conversations and avoid them—and that's a first-class ticket to being alone.

*Scan this QR Code to get the companion book that will help discover some social and physical damages of overthinking.

However, anxiety can really throw a wrench in your ability to communicate effectively with your partner: "It takes a lot of mental energy to hold a conversation, even if it doesn't seem like it. So it should come as little surprise that when your mind is overwhelmed with anxiety it can impair your ability to communicate" (Abraham, 2020). To genuinely converse with others, we need more cognitive capacity than we realize. This is due to the brain's need to listen to information, comprehend it, process it, and come up with a proper response. Learning that surprised me as well, but when you think about it, it's not strange that people with anxiety find it difficult to communicate owing to the continual labor their brain is putting in due to overthinking and tension. Any relationship will suffer as a result of this.

Negative Effect on Problem-Solving in Relationships

Do you ever feel like bringing up an issue that you're supposed to discuss with your partner would result in conflict, so you ignore it? "Does telling your partner that you don't want to go to their family for the holidays feel like it might explode into an emotional drama?" (Blue, 2018). If so, this is rather typical. Conflicts are a normal part of life, and people who suffer from anxiety are no exception. However, avoiding an issue out of fear of having an argument is destructive to a relationship—such pent-up emotions will inevitably manifest in other ways.

Recognizing and confronting difficulties head-on promotes a good partnership.

Unfortunately, anxious people struggle with confrontation; they often rehearse the entire conversation in their head hundreds of times before it actually happens, which leads to a worry of things going horribly wrong, so they avoid having the conversation altogether. The mistake they make here is that by not bringing it up, they deprive their partner of a say in the matter. Another reason those with anxiety delay resolving problems is the emotional baggage or drama that comes with it. Anxious people find it difficult to communicate their emotions and thus avoid anything involving emotional turmoil.

When Trust and Intimacy Issues Come In

It is natural for trust concerns to arise in a partnership with inadequate communication. Intimacy anxiety—the dread of being overly emotionally involved or attached to someone—is quite common. Anxious people are terrified of being judged and criticized by others, even in their relationships, and therefore they avoid becoming emotionally involved with others. Anxious people are often distrustful, and considering that relationships are built on trust, having a partner who doesn't trust you doesn't sit well with most people. Those with anxiety who have trust and intimacy issues are also more likely to be in relationships that are shallow.

Having trust issues is one of the negative effects of anxiety on a relationship. It is characterized by always assuming the worst, being suspicious about everything, distancing yourself from your partner, etc. It's very hard for an anxious individual to trust someone, especially when they've been hurt in the past; due to their tendency to overthink, they never really forget those part hurts, and then they become insecure about everything and everyone. They'd rather distance themselves from everyone because they're scared of being hurt or let down, or of not being good enough.

The Need for Emotional Resilience

Emotional resilience can be defined as the ability to cope with difficult situations, adversity, and trauma. In this harsh modern-day world where making someone cry helps you win points on social media and emotionally assaulting someone implies you're an "alpha male," it's critical to develop emotional resilience. This helps us shrug off cruel remarks, backstabbing, and many other emotional assaults. We have no control over what happens to us, so being emotionally resilient will help us adapt, shrug it off, and bounce back to a state of wellbeing.

Nelson Mandela once said, "The greatest glory in living lies not in never falling, but in rising every time we fall." To rise after adversity and trauma does not imply that we do not feel anything; it simply means that we have a thicker skin or recover faster when we fall. It means that we recognize that we have been harmed and broken, yet we do not lose our strength and instead continue on. Being emotionally resilient will help you survive even the most ferocious storms.

Stress is a key cause of anxiety, and being emotionally resilient will help those with anxiety develop positive coping strategies for stressful events, lowering their likelihood of becoming unwell as a result of the stress and overthinking. Overthinking is stressful on the human body and has a number of negative consequences, but having a coping method for whatever life throws our way can help us bounce back and keep going—and the more we do this, the easier it is to bounce back and recover from terrible circumstances. Individuals with anxiety who develop emotional resilience begin to think differently and more positively rather than worrying over the past (which I'm sure, in many cases, we'd like to forget). It enables us to progress and heal, and it shapes us into better versions of ourselves.

To do this, we must acknowledge that our ideas influence our actions, which is the first step in developing emotional resilience. Following acceptance, the next step is to find balance by focusing on the positive aspects of life rather than the negative.

Reasons we need to be emotionally resilient:

1. Reduced anxiety: Being emotionally resilient enables us, especially those who struggle with anxiety, to focus on the positive aspects of life rather than linger on the

negative. It transforms our mode of thinking and helps us uncover our willpower. Overcoming adversity boosts self-esteem and confidence, which reduces worry. It allows us to put aside our continual worrying and focus on methods to improve ourselves.

2. Risk of physical sickness is reduced: Stress weakens the human body, making it more prone to illness and infection; being resilient in stressful situations considerably reduces this risk. Stress aggravates preexisting medical issues, and emotional resilience helps us relax and find constructive answers to unpleasant situations.

3. Longer-lasting and healthier relationships: Being emotionally resilient benefits everyone, not just anxious people, because the ability to accept that not everything in life will go our way, and that we have to bounce back, shrug it off, and get back into the ring, leads to healthier and stronger relationships. Having a partner who supports you increases your chances of success. When both partners are resilient, they may be able to concentrate on the positives while learning from the negatives. It also prevents people struggling with anxiety and overthinking from isolating themselves from those who love them when they face difficulties;

instead, it improves their thinking and communication skills and helps them form stronger bonds.

MAIN IDEAS

Let's return to Daniel's situation as discussed at the beginning of this chapter. As Daniel's worry and overthinking intensified, his relationship with Lauren began to suffer. His constant preoccupation with small details and worst-case scenarios left little room for spontaneity, joy, and connection. While he was initially admired for his responsible nature, his excessive worry started to overshadow his positive qualities. Instead of being present and enjoying the moment with Lauren, his mind was consumed by overanalyzing every aspect of their relationship.

As time went on, Daniel's inability to switch off his worries created a growing distance between him and Lauren. Despite her attempts to reassure him and offer support, his mind remained fixated on imaginary problems and potential pitfalls. The lack of peace and relaxation within Daniel's mind made it challenging for him to truly appreciate and cherish the love they shared. Ultimately, the strain caused by his constant worrying became too much for their relationship to bear, leading to their breakup.

Daniel's experience highlights the destructive nature of excessive worry and overthinking in relationships. It serves as a reminder that finding a balance between responsibility and letting go of unnecessary anxiety is crucial for fostering healthy connections with others.

Anxiety and overthinking can have a negative impact on the dynamics of a relationship, affecting both persons involved. Anxiety frequently causes a state of perpetual tension, prompting romantic partners to doubt themselves, each other, and the stability of their connection. This can lead them to excessively examine every element of their interactions, resulting in hypersensitivity to perceived threats and a lack of trust. As a result, communication may become strained, intimacy may suffer, and tensions may flare up. The negative cycle of anxiety and overthinking can create a poisonous environment, weakening the relationship's basis of trust and emotional connection.

Furthermore, anxiety and overthinking can have a negative impact on a person's wellbeing, self-esteem, and mental health in a relationship. Constant worrying and ruminating can result in increased stress, sleep difficulties, and even medical problems. Individuals may become fixated on negative ideas and worst-case scenarios, making it difficult to appreciate the current moment or adopt a cheerful attitude. This self-centered attitude can also lead to greater demands for reassurance and affirmation from their partner, putting further strain on the relationship. If not addressed and managed successfully, anxiety and overthinking can contribute to a cycle of unhappiness, insecurity, and instability, damaging the relationship's general health and durability.

WORKBOOK THREE

Section 1: Self-Reflection

1. Describe your own experience with anxiety and overthinking in relationships. How does it manifest for you?

2. Reflect on how anxiety and overthinking have affected your past and current relationships. What negative patterns or challenges have you noticed?

3. Explore the possible underlying causes of your anxiety and overthinking in relationships. Are there any past experiences or personal beliefs that contribute to these patterns?

Section 2: Identifying the Impact

4. How do anxiety and overthinking affect your communication with your partner? Do you tend to overanalyze their words or actions? How does this impact the quality of your conversations?

5. Reflect on the level of trust in your relationship. Have anxiety and overthinking affected your ability to trust your partner fully? How does this impact your overall connection?

6. Consider the impact of anxiety and overthinking on intimacy and vulnerability. Do you find it difficult to

be open and emotionally available due to these patterns? How does it affect your ability to connect on a deeper level?

Section 3: Communication and Conflict Resolution

7. Practice active listening exercises to improve your communication skills. This can include paraphrasing, summarizing, and asking open-ended questions.

Section 4: Self-Care and Anxiety Management

8. Identify self-care activities that help alleviate anxiety and promote emotional wellbeing. This could include exercise, journaling, or engaging in hobbies.

9. Seek professional help if needed. Research therapists or counselors specializing in anxiety and relationship issues. Consider reaching out for support and guidance.

Section 5: Building Trust and Nurturing the Relationship

10. Reflect on your partner's perspective and practice empathy. Put yourself in their shoes and consider how your anxiety and overthinking may affect them. Discuss your findings with your partner.

Conclusion:

Reflect on the insights gained from this workbook. Consider the changes you want to make in your approach to anxiety and overthinking in your relationship.

PART TWO

Connect More to Love More

In this second part, you'll be introduced to strategies by which you can prevent relationship anxiety and overthinking from ruining your relationship. This part consists of discussions on the following topics:

- Loosening the anxiety thread loop
- Deepening your connections
- Building healthy habits

You'll find valuable resources and guidance to overcome the challenges of relationship anxiety and overthinking. In focusing on loosening the anxiety thread loop, you'll learn techniques to interrupt negative thought patterns and cultivate a more balanced perspective. Additionally, you'll explore strategies for deepening your connection with your partner, fostering trust, and enhancing emotional intimacy. Through building healthy habits, you'll discover actionable steps to create a solid foundation for a thriving relationship.

Embrace this opportunity to empower yourself with the knowledge and skills to navigate relationship challenges with resilience and create a more harmonious and fulfilling partnership. Enjoy!

CHAPTER FOUR

Loosening the Anxiety Thread Loop

"Cast your burden on the Lord, And He shall sustain you; He shall never permit the righteous to be moved."

—Proverbs 55:22

"Anxiety is a whispering thread that tries to suffocate our dreams. Don't let it silence your potential. Gather the courage to break free and weave a tapestry of fulfillment."

—Roy T. Bennett

In the bustling city of New York, there was a man named Matt. He was a diligent and ambitious individual, but his drive for success often came at the cost of his peace of mind. In his relationships, Matt had a tendency to overanalyze every interaction, constantly second-guessing both himself and his partner and fearing rejection.

One day, Matt met Lily, a free-spirited artist with a radiant smile that could melt his worries away. As they embarked on their journey of love and companionship, Matt's anxiety began to tighten its grip, threatening to suffocate their connection and ruin their relationship. Sensitive to his distress, Lily, with her compassionate nature, decided to address the issue. She took Matt's hands and whispered, "Matt, I see the beauty in your heart, and I believe in us. Let's break free from the chains of anxiety and overthinking together. Trust in our love, trust in me." They began to work on exercises that could help Matt with his anxiety and also help Lily to become more patient and understanding.

Anxiety is a mental health problem that affects people all over the world. It is characterized by dread and agitation, which can seriously disrupt our daily life and general wellbeing. Academics and mental health specialists are constantly investigating methods to alleviate anxiety symptoms and make patients feel better. One intriguing concept that is gaining traction is known as "loosening the anxiety thread loop." The goal of this strategy is to figure out how to stop the cycle of anxious thoughts and behaviors that keeps us in a state of anxiety.

Neuroplasticity: It's Possible to Rewire Your Anxious Brain

Neuroplasticity is a fancy term that basically means our brains can change and adapt throughout our lives; it's "the brain's ability to rewire itself by paving new neural pathways when it feels the need to adapt" (Sharma, 2022). While it's true that the brain is "a beautiful thing" and "a complex learning machine to help you navigate life's many challenges" (Lebow, 2021), it also serves the role of protecting us from danger, and as a result it can become "confused, and to keep us safe, it can make us feel more anxious and alert" (Sharma, 2022). There is good news, though: "Your brain has the ability to rewire itself, making new connections between neurons and remapping the information you've gathered so far" (Lebow, 2021).

"By paving new neural pathways and creating new connections between neurons, we can train our brains to reduce anxiety and response" (Sharma, 2022). For example, if someone suffers a brain injury or a stroke and loses their motor skills, physical therapy can potentially help that person to regain those skills. This is due to neuroplasticity. And guess what? This doesn't only apply to physical skills; we can also "train [our] brain to promote positive thinking that can help improve [our] mental health" (Sharma, 2022).

It was once believed that the structure and function of the brain were fixed and unchanging after a certain age. However, new research has shown that the brain is pliable and capable of rewiring itself even in maturity. This notion of neuroplasticity offers hope for those who suffer from anxiety since it implies that it is feasible to rewire an anxious brain and lessen the impact of worry on one's life.

So, how does neuroplasticity work? Well, our brain's neurons can form new connections and adjust themselves based on our experiences and the things happening around us. If we keep activating certain neural pathways, those connections get stronger. On the other hand, if we stop using certain pathways, they weaken. For people with anxiety, this means that patterns of anxious thoughts and behaviors become deeply ingrained in the brain, making it harder to break free of the anxiety.

Identifying Negative Thought Patterns

Negative thinking happens at an unconscious level and is often the root cause of some of our negative behavior (Swaby, 2019). Negative thought patterns can also be referred to as cognitive distortions. By becoming aware of these patterns, we can challenge and reframe them, ultimately reducing anxiety and promoting healthier relationship dynamics. Types of cognitive distortions include:

1. Catastrophizing: This involves exaggerating the significance of events, such as when you make a mistake (Stress & Development Lab, Harvard University). For example, someone might catastrophize by believing that a minor disagreement with their partner will inevitably lead to the end of the relationship. Essentially, catastrophizing is taking in the situation and coming to the (inaccurate) conclusion that "the worst outcome is going to happen to us" (Roncero, 2021).

2. Selective abstraction: This is "when we pay attention to a certain piece of information and ignore the rest of the information and context" (Roncero, 2021). Similar to

catastrophizing, it involves magnifying certain negative elements and discounting positive or neutral aspects, leading to distorted perceptions and increased anxiety. In the context of a relationship, selective abstraction could manifest as fixating on a negative comment from your partner while disregarding the overall positive aspects of the partnership.

3. Personalization: This involves assuming excessive responsibility for negative events or outcomes, even when they are beyond one's control. In the context of a relationship, personalization can manifest as taking on the full burden of a problem, believing that you are solely responsible for the difficulties your partner is experiencing. For instance, someone may blame themselves entirely for a relationship conflict, disregarding external factors or the other person's role.

Identifying negative thought patterns is a crucial step in reducing anxiety and overthinking in your relationship. By recognizing cognitive distortions such as catastrophizing, selective abstraction, and personalization, you can challenge these negative patterns and cultivate more balanced and realistic thinking.

Challenging Your Negative Thoughts: What Works

Negative thoughts, or cognitive distortions, are "a form of unhealthy self-talk" and "can quickly consume all of our thoughts" (High Focus Treatment Centers, 2021). So what can we do about it? "The key to changing your negative thoughts is to understand how you think now (and the problems that result), then use strategies to change these thoughts or make them have less of an effect" (Cuncic, 2023).

Negative thoughts have a way of sneaking in, messing with our heads, and making us doubt everyone—including our partner, the person we're meant to trust wholeheartedly. They really do have a way of throwing us off-balance, especially when it comes to relationships. But breathe a sigh of relief: we are more than able to challenge those thoughts and regain control *through Christ Who strengthens us*. By finding effective methods and strategies to tackle our negative thinking, we can break free from the grip of anxiety and build healthier, more beautiful relationships.

So, what really works when it comes to challenging negative thoughts?

1. Identifying and understanding: The first and most crucial step is to identify the negative thought pattern(s) you tend to experience. There are multiple patterns, including personalization, catastrophizing, selective abstraction, and black-and-white thinking, among

many others. It is crucial to identify and understand these thought patterns. Read about them and about the kinds of emotions they bring up, as well as what triggers them.

2. Acceptance: I am sure this sounds confusing, doesn't it? *Robert, you just said we should and are more than able to challenge these negative thought patterns. Why then are you telling me to accept them?* Because you are accepting the thoughts for what they are: thoughts, and not facts. A negative thought is just something your mind has made up and not your reality.

3. Give yourself a break: It's so very easy to blame ourselves for anything that goes wrong. This thought pattern is called personalization and, as explained earlier, it involves assuming excessive responsibility for negative events or outcomes, even when they're beyond your control. In your relationship, it could manifest as taking responsibility for disagreements, or assuming any problem in your relationship is all your fault. This not only tears you down as a person, it could make you unnecessarily willing to stay in a wrong relationship, or could make your partner feel suffocated and manipulated. Giving yourself a break does not relieve you of all responsibility, but it involves accepting the fact that you are human, and that everyone makes mistakes (including you and your partner). Giving

yourself a break can be both physical and mental. Physically, it may involve taking time off from work, engaging in leisure activities, or simply allowing yourself to rest and recover. Mentally, it entails giving your mind a break from constant thinking and worrying. It can also involve practicing self-care, disconnecting from the world for a while, and asking for help.

4. Mindfulness: "Mindfulness is the practice of gently focusing your awareness on the present moment over and over again" (Hoshaw, 2020). The mind is like a child with a sugar rush, always running wild. Mindfulness involves taking control over your mind, rather than letting it run roughshod over you. You can practice mindfulness by carrying out simple daily exercises like cooking or gardening and informing your mind about what you're doing at that particular moment. This helps you to focus on the present moment rather than being carried away by thoughts that most likely do not relate to that moment. You could also start a thought journal; writing down your thoughts (especially the ones that seem overwhelming) can be a great way to release the tension and stress that typically come with the negativity. Why not add Bible verses to your thoughts as you write them down? This is a great way to counter the negative thinking, and it

could help you to focus on what God says rather than what your mind says.

5. Gratitude: Yes, gratitude. Gratitude can be a great way of challenging your negative thoughts. Gratitude generally provides a countereffect to overthinking and negative thinking. Thinking about what you do have and being grateful to God can help you overcome those negative and ungrateful thoughts. Likewise, in your relationship, being grateful for your partner and reminiscing on the beautiful moments you've had together can help you overcome negative thoughts, doubts, and fears.*

---

* **Scan this QR Code** and start developing and maintaining a healthy mindset now by using the tips from the Part IV of the *"Enough Overthinking."*

Practicing Positive Self-Talk

"No hard feelings, but I'm going to need you to leave."

Self-talk can be defined as "the internal dialogue a person has with themselves" and "is a natural cognitive process" (Richards, 2022). Everyone naturally engages in self-talk throughout the day (Morris, 2016), but it's up to you whether that self-talk is positive and encouraging or negative and discouraging (Holland, 2020). Negative self-talk is an extremely damaging way of talking to yourself. It affects your emotions, leading to even more damaging self-talk and behavior. Essentially, it is a prominent component of the vicious anxiety cycle. For example, you may repeatedly tell yourself that you can't pass a difficult exam—and then, when you do fail, you say, "I knew it." And on it goes.

Now, please note that "positive self-talk doesn't mean ignoring the negative or unpleasant aspects of life. Instead, it's flipping the narrative so that you can approach these issues in a more positive and productive way" (DPS Staff, 2021). It involves creating "an internal dialogue that makes a person feel good about themselves" (Richards, 2022). If you cultivate positive self-talk, it can help you develop effective ways of coping with and letting go of your anxiety and overthinking. Methods by which you can practice positive self-talk include:

1. Recognize negative thinking: The first and most crucial step is to identify and recognize your negative thinking. As explained earlier, there are three major types of negative thought patterns:

   - Personalization—taking absolute responsibility for any negative event that occurs

   - Catastrophizing—exaggerating issues and imagining the worst possible outcome

   - Selective abstraction—paying attention to negative aspects of an issue and ignoring other factors

Recognizing your negative thinking can make it easier to turn your thoughts into positive ones. For example, if you begin to have wild thoughts about your partner cheating on you just because they weren't able to pick up your call, recognizing your negative thinking at that moment can help you convert "*Is she cheating on me?*" into "*She's probably busy. She'll call back as soon as she can.*"

2. Treat yourself the way you would treat a friend: If your friend were to come to you with unfounded and irrational suspicions about their partner cheating, wouldn't you speak sense to them calmly but sternly? This is what I mean by treating yourself the way you would treat a dear friend. Kindly but sternly, talk to and treat yourself better.

3. Make self-care a priority: This is an essential step in practicing positive self-talk. Taking care of your physical, emotional, and mental wellbeing can greatly influence your internal dialogue. Make sure you're getting enough sleep, take breaks when needed, and engage in activities that can help you unwind and recharge. Learn to say no when necessary, and prioritize activities that can help you and your partner relax together and bond with each other. Draw boundaries as well if you feel they are needed.

4. Limit your exposure to negativity: It could be a friend, it could be social media. Whatever you feel is contributing to your negative thoughts concerning yourself and your relationship should be removed from

your life. Deleting certain social media apps from your phone, or ghosting that particular person who never has anything positive to say, is not too great a sacrifice to make for the sake of your mental wellbeing and relationship.

5. Change your vocabulary: Self-talk is your inner dialogue, right? So what words do you tend to use when speaking to yourself? Changing your vocabulary involves being watchful and cautious with your words, and consciously using positive words and sentences rather than negative ones.

6. Practice positive affirmations: Posting positive affirmations and Bible verses about yourself around your room or in visible places around your space can be a great way to challenge negative self-talk.

7. Laugh: Learn to find the humor in situations around you. I'm not saying you should never take things seriously, but learn to let certain things roll off your back and just laugh. Laugh at yourself, at funny situations, and with your partner.

Reversing the 4 Stages of Anxiety

The stages of anxiety are described by numerous theories and frameworks. The "anxiety cycle" described by Clark and Beck (2010) is a widely used model that describes four stages: trigger, assessment, physical response, and behavioral response. These stages help in developing an understanding of the progression and manifestation of anxiety symptoms.

The trigger is the starting point of the anxiety cycle. External occurrences or internal thoughts, memories, or feelings that cause anxiety are examples of triggers. Triggers can differ greatly amongst people and can include specific situations, social interactions, perceived threats, or even anticipatory anxiety. A trigger could be a word your partner says or their ignoring a call in your presence, for example. Triggers start the assessment process, which leads to the second stage of anxiety.

The trigger is mentally assessed in the second stage. This stage involves interpreting the trigger in regard to personal significance, threat, or danger. Cognitive assessments include beliefs, thoughts, and perceptions regarding the trigger, oneself, and one's ability to deal.

The third stage of the anxiety cycle involves the physical response. This stage encompasses the physiological reactions that accompany anxiety, such as increased heart rate, rapid breathing, muscle tension, sweating, and heightened alertness (Clark & Beck, 2010).

These physical symptoms are caused by the body's natural stress reaction, often known as the "fight-or-flight" response, which prepares a person to deal with perceived threats or hazards.

The behavioral response is the final stage of the anxiety cycle. This stage includes the anxiety-related avoidance behaviors that people participate in. Our behavioral responses to anxiety can differ depending on the nature of the anxiety. To relieve anxiety, some people engage in behaviors such as avoiding social situations or specific triggers, while others participate in safety-seeking activities or rituals. These activities are intended to regulate or relieve anxiety symptoms, but they can also reinforce and extend the anxiety cycle over time.

It is important to note that the stages of anxiety described above are not necessarily linear or isolated. They can interact and influence each other, creating a cyclic pattern (i.e., the anxiety cycle). For example, behavioral responses (such as avoidance) may reinforce cognitive assessments (such as confirming the perceived threat) and prolong the anxiety cycle (Clark & Beck, 2010).

Now, how do we reverse or counteract the effects of these stages? While reversing the four stages of anxiety may be difficult, there are methods that can assist us in managing and reducing anxiety symptoms. These strategies address each stage of the cycle, with the goal of breaking the pattern and encouraging a more adaptive response to triggers.

To address the trigger stage, individuals can benefit from identifying and understanding their specific triggers. Keeping a trigger diary or participating in self-reflection might help you identify thoughts and events that can cause anxiety. Cognitive restructuring approaches, such as challenging irrational thoughts or beliefs related to triggers, might assist in reframing negative interpretations and reducing perceived threats (Hofmann, 2011).

Individuals might concentrate on improving their cognitive assessments of triggers throughout the assessment stage. CBT (cognitive behavioral therapy) is a well-established strategy that focuses on recognizing and addressing erroneous thoughts and beliefs that lead to anxiety (Beck, 2011). Examining evidence for and against anxious beliefs, establishing more balanced ideas, and producing alternative explanations for triggers can all be part of this process. Acceptance-based therapies, such as Acceptance and Commitment Therapy (ACT), can also assist individuals in developing acceptance and willingness to feel anxiety while aligning their actions with their beliefs (Hayes et al., 2012).

Managing the physiological symptoms linked with anxiety is part of addressing the physical reaction stage. Regular exercise and relaxing activities like meditation can help control the body's stress response and promote general well-being (Rosenbaum et al., 2014).

In the behavioral response stage, individuals can work on gradually confronting and approaching feared situations through exposure-based techniques. Gradual exposure therapy allows individuals to confront anxiety-provoking situations in a controlled and systematic manner, gradually reducing avoidance behaviors (Choy et al., 2007). This can be accomplished by either imaginal exposure (mentally imagining the feared situation) or in vivo exposure (actually participating in the feared situation). With time, patience, and practice, individuals can gain confidence and minimize anxiety-related avoidance behaviors.

It is essential that I point out that reversing the anxiety stages will require relentless work, patience, and support. Working with a skilled mental health practitioner, such as a psychologist or therapist specializing in anxiety disorders, can provide greater help and support in applying these strategies to your life.

The 4 Rs That Work

Psychologist Jeffrey Schwartz created 4 Rs to assist in reducing anxiety (Pinnacle Recovery, 2019). They offer a way by which you can distance yourself from "an anxiety spiral" (Shea, 2021), acting as a framework for managing and overcoming anxiety. The 4 Rs are Relabel, Reattribute, Refocus, and Revalue. Let's explore each of these in more detail:

1. Relabel: The first step is to label what you're dealing with (Shea, 2021). Recognize that what you're experiencing is a manifestation of your anxiety (Burns, 1999). Labeling the issue can "put some of the power back in your hands, turning a rogue wave into something a little more manageable, or at least

identifiable" (Shea, 2021). This allows you to separate yourself from the overwhelming emotions and gain a sense of control.

2. Reattribute: Next up, it's important to challenge and reframe the negative thoughts and beliefs that accompany your anxiety. Instead of attributing the feelings to personal failures or weaknesses, it's crucial to recognize that they are primarily driven by anxiety itself. You can detach your identity from the anxiety and acquire a more realistic perspective by reattributing the feelings to anxiety. While there might be other contributors to your anxiety, you need to realize that your current anxiety is due to those factors and not to your flaws as a person.

3. Refocus: Refocusing your mind involves consciously directing your thoughts away from your anxiety to something more positive and productive. It could involve engaging in activities you enjoy, calling a friend for a quick chitchat, or focusing on the present moment. Refocusing helps break the cycle of overthinking and excessive worry associated with anxiety.

4. Revalue: It's now time to revalue. Ask yourself questions about what could have happened if you had given in to your anxiety. By challenging negative beliefs

and assumptions associated with anxiety, you can reduce its influence over your thoughts and actions. Recognize that anxiety does not define you as a person and that you have the power to revalue its importance.

Implementing the four Rs is a continuous process that requires patience. Although progress is not always straightforward, you will be able to gradually let go of anxiety and overthinking by relabeling, reattributing, refocusing, and revaluing these patterns, thereby creating a healthy relationship built on trust, communication, and emotional wellbeing.

The Role of Self-Awareness

Self-awareness "gives us the power to influence outcomes"; it "helps us become better decision-makers and gives us more self-confidence" (Aronov-Jacoby, 2022). In the words of psychologists Shelley Duval and Robert Wicklund, it is "the ability to focus on yourself and how your actions, thoughts, or emotions do or don't align with your internal standards. If you're highly self-aware, you can objectively evaluate yourself, manage your emotions, align your behavior with your values, and understand correctly how others perceive you" (cited in Betz, 2022). Simply put, "Self-awareness is knowing yourself. It is understanding your feelings, motives, goals, and biases" (Soken-Huberty, 2023).

Self-awareness is essential for letting go of anxiety and overthinking in your relationships. It's all about developing a deep awareness of your own ideas, feelings, and habits, allowing you to gain crucial insights into what causes your anxiety and how it shows up in your relationships, allowing you to address and manage it better.

Being able to recognize and examine your anxious thoughts is a crucial element of self-awareness. When anxiety begins to seep in, simply noticing and being aware of these feelings and thoughts allows you to separate from them and restore control.

Self-awareness also assists you in recognizing how your anxiety affects your relationships. It enables you to observe how it influences your communication, emotional availability, and capacity to trust and connect with your spouse or partner. This awareness is effective because it allows you to differentiate between what is genuine and the distorted impressions caused by anxiety.

It takes time and effort to develop self-awareness. It entails paying attention to your thoughts, feelings, and behaviors in various settings, particularly during difficult times in your relationships. Self-reflection activities, writing, and counseling may all be extremely beneficial in increasing your self-awareness and developing the skills you need to handle anxiety and overthinking in your relationships.

Cognitive Restructuring for Negative Thoughts

Cognitive restructuring is a cornerstone of cognitive behavioral therapy (Stanborough, 2020). It is a technique mostly used to change our thought patterns. It can be used to replace negative thoughts with more positive and balanced ones that do not lead to anxiety.

The first thing to do is identify your negative thoughts: are you catastrophizing, personalizing, or thinking in terms of selective abstraction? After recognizing these patterns, the next thing to do is to examine the root factors. Rationally and calmly, identify the triggers. This leads to the next step, which involves examining whether there's any truth to your thoughts. After this, consciously and purposefully replace these thoughts with more balanced ones that relate to the situation but do not cause panic or anxiety.

How CBT Works

According to the UK's National Health Service (2022), "Cognitive behavioural therapy (CBT) is a talking therapy that can help you manage your problems by changing the way you think and behave." This technique is highly effective in allowing us to change our thought patterns in order to change our behavior (Davis, 2023).

The recognition that our thoughts, feelings, and behaviors are all interconnected is a core principle of CBT. Our thoughts have the ability to influence how we feel and act, and vice versa.

Individuals suffering from anxiety and overthinking are prone to erroneous thinking patterns defined by negative assumptions, catastrophic interpretations, or excessive worry about future outcomes.

CBT helps people become aware of their incorrect thoughts and challenge the veracity of those thoughts. The therapist helps the client to discover and assess their automatic thoughts, looking at the evidence for and against them, followed by replacing irrational or negative thoughts with more balanced and realistic ones (Beck, 2011).

For example, if a person suffering from anxiety has the automatic thought, "My partner will leave me if I make a mistake," the therapist will assist them in analyzing the evidence for this assumption. They could talk about previous experiences, the partner's actions, and alternative theories. The client begins to reframe their thinking as a result of this process, seeing that their anxiety-driven beliefs are not supported by reliable evidence.

CBT focuses on changing behaviors that lead to anxiety and overthinking in addition to addressing thoughts. Individuals are encouraged to conduct behavioral experiments and put new coping techniques into practice in real-life settings.

CBT also acknowledges the impact of environmental and interpersonal factors on anxiety and overthinking. The therapist may explore relationship dynamics, communication patterns, and social support networks with the client in order to identify areas that require growth. This technique teaches people how their connections can both contribute to and ease anxiety and overthinking.

It's important to remember that CBT is a therapy in which the therapist and the client work together, and it is also short-term and time-bound. The client must participate actively in the therapy process, working with their therapist to develop goals and practice new skills. Treatment approaches and strategies are then applied in real life, helping the client apply what they have learned and continue improvement outside of treatment sessions.

Employing Graded Exposure

Graded exposure therapy focuses on breaking the link between your anxiety trigger and your brain's reaction that causes the physiological anxiety response (Hutchinson, 2022). As its name suggests, it involves gradually exposing yourself to feared situations and/or stimuli. A hierarchy is created, and you start by facing the smaller fears, slowly working up to the larger ones. It's quite different from flooding, which is another exposure technique that involves exposing yourself to the feared situations and/or stimuli all at once. Flooding is not often used, as it's difficult for most individuals to manage that level of exposure.

During the graded exposure process, the client is encouraged to apply the coping techniques and strategies already learned. Continuous exposure in this form helps the client to slowly but surely overcome their fears and anxiety-causing thoughts.

Using gradual exposure requires patience and perseverance. It is typical to feel some discomfort and worry during the process, but with each successful exposure, you can build resilience and acquire more control over your anxious thoughts and actions, including the ones that show up in your relationship.

Remember that the purpose of graded exposure therapy is to build a healthier relationship with anxiety rather than to eradicate all anxious thoughts. It is about learning to accept and regulate your anxiety while remaining involved in meaningful and happy relationships.

Neuroplasticity Exercises That Work

Neuroplasticity is our brain's ability "to change and adapt," and research shows that it's "a fundamental part of keeping cognitively fit" (Sugden, 2022). Your brain is like a muscle: the more you exercise it, the stronger it gets. When your brain processes new information, neurons fire, new pathways form, and the malleable brain alters its shape and structure (Thompson, 2022); isn't that incredible? For many years, it was believed that we were born with a finite number of neurons, and that as we grew older, these cells died—however, recent research has brought to light the beautiful realization that our brains can continue to change and develop throughout our adult years. Picture your brain as an interconnected interplay of neurons and pathways. These neurons and pathways light up as you use them; for example, thinking about the word "book" puts to work every neuron and pathway connected with the word "book." If you begin to learn a new language, new pathways are formed, and when you then think about the word "book," the new pathways connecting "book" to the new language are activated.

Improving your neuroplasticity has also been shown to reduce the incidence of age-related cognitive illnesses, so it's incredibly beneficial to engage in neuroplasticity exercises (Sugden, 2022).

Examples of neuroplasticity exercises include:

1. Learning a new language: As we discussed in the example above, studying a language is a fantastic opportunity to develop your neuroplasticity; "every word is an opportunity for a new neural connection to be created in the brain" (Sugden, 2022).

2. Learning how to play a musical instrument: Acquiring a new skill with a musical instrument "may increase connectivity between brain regions and help form new neural networks" (Ackerman, 2018). Additionally, studies show that learning a musical instrument lowers

our risk of cognitive impairment later in life (Sugden, 2022).

3. Learning a physical skill: Working on a new physical skill, such as juggling, is a great way to increase your brain's neuroplasticity as you create new pathways related to the connection between vision and movement (Sugden, 2022).

4. Playing stimulating games like chess: A mentally stimulating game, such as chess, "has endless potential for neuroplasticity" (Thompson, 2022).

5. Exercise: Of course, we all know that exercise is good for us on a physical level, and it can reduce anxiety and overthinking in its own right, but guess what? It can also increase neuroplasticity because it actually changes the structure of the brain (Sugden, 2022).

6. Non-dominant hand exercises: Practicing skills with your non-dominant hand also helps your brain to form new connections (Ackerman, 2018). For example, you could attempt to write a sentence or brush your teeth with your non-dominant hand. One expert suggests doing these exercises "while balancing on one leg for a double neuroplasticity bonus" (Thompson, 2022).

By actively engaging in neuroplasticity exercises such as these, you can reshape your neural pathways and reduce your tendency to be anxious and overthink about your relationship.

Cognitive Restructuring Worksheets

The following worksheets are designed to help you practice cognitive restructuring techniques and loosen the anxiety thread loop in your relationship. By challenging and reframing your negative thoughts, you can gain a more balanced perspective and reduce anxiety and overthinking. Take your time to work through each exercise, and feel free to add any additional insights or reflections as you progress. Remember, this is a process of self-discovery and growth. Let's begin!

Worksheet 1: Identifying Negative Thought Patterns
Instructions:

- Reflect on your recent experiences in relationships.

- Write down any recurring negative thoughts or beliefs that come to mind.

- Consider the specific situations or triggers that tend to activate these negative thoughts.

- Take note of the emotions associated with these thoughts.

Example:

- Negative Thought: "I'm not good enough for my partner."

- Triggering Situation: When my partner spends time with their friends without me.

- Emotions: Inadequacy, insecurity, jealousy

Worksheet 2: Cognitive Restructuring
Instructions:

- Choose one negative thought identified in Worksheet 1 to work with.

- Write down the evidence that supports this negative thought.

- Now, challenge the negative thought by finding alternative evidence or perspectives that contradict it.

- Generate a more balanced and realistic thought or belief based on the evidence you have gathered.

- Write down the new thought or belief and consider how it might affect your feelings and behaviors in your relationship.

Example:

- Negative Thought: "I'm not good enough for my partner."

- Supporting Evidence: Sometimes I make mistakes and feel insecure.

- Challenging Evidence: My partner tells me they love and appreciate me. I have qualities that they admire.

- New Thought: "I have my own unique strengths and qualities that make me worthy of love and affection."

- Impact on Feelings and Behaviors: This new belief boosts my self-esteem and allows me to feel more secure in my relationship.

Worksheet 3: Applying Cognitive Restructuring
Instructions:

- Recall a recent situation in which you experienced anxiety or overthinking in your relationship.

- Write down the negative thoughts that emerged from that situation.

- Apply the cognitive restructuring process by challenging the negative thought with alternative evidence and generating a more balanced thought.

- Reflect on how this new thought might have influenced your emotions and behaviors in that situation.

By practicing these exercises regularly, you can develop a more balanced and realistic perspective, promoting greater emotional wellbeing and healthier connections. Remember, change takes time and effort, so be patient with yourself.

CBT Worksheets

Worksheet 1: Recognizing Negative Thoughts
Instructions:

- Reflect on your recent experiences in your relationship(s).

- Write down any negative thoughts or beliefs that have contributed to your anxiety and overthinking.

- Identify the triggers or specific situations that tend to activate these negative thoughts.

- Note the emotions or physical sensations associated with these thoughts.

Worksheet 2: Challenging the Thoughts
Instructions:

- Choose one negative thought identified in Worksheet 1 to focus on.

- Write down the evidence that supports this negative thought.

- Now, challenge the negative thought by examining the evidence against it.

- Generate a more realistic and balanced thought based on the evidence you have gathered.

- Write down the new thought and consider how it might influence your emotions and behaviors in your relationship.

Worksheet 3: Behavior Experiment
Instructions:

- Identify a specific anxiety-provoking situation in your relationship.

- Write down the negative thought associated with that situation.

- Create a behavioral experiment to test the validity of the negative thought.

- Plan and carry out the experiment, noting any observations or new insights gained.

- Reflect on the results and consider how they challenge or reshape the negative thought.

Remember to practice these techniques consistently and be patient with yourself as you navigate the journey towards a healthier relationship.

MAIN IDEAS

Let's return to Matt and Lily from the opening of this chapter. Through their shared commitment and support for one another, the couple embarked on a journey of growth and healing. They recognized that overcoming anxiety and overthinking required both individual effort and a strong bond between them. They challenged their negative thoughts by engaging in cognitive restructuring, encouraging one another to replace self-doubt with self-compassion and realistic perspectives. Additionally, they embraced graded exposure therapy, gradually facing their fears and insecurities as a team and celebrating each small victory along the way. As they navigated this path together, their love and trust blossomed, and the grip of anxiety slowly loosened its hold.

When it comes to letting go of anxiety and overthinking in your relationship, loosening the anxiety thread loop is crucial. By actively incorporating strategies like cognitive restructuring, graded exposure, gratitude practice, and behavioral activation, you have the power to reshape your thoughts, face your fears step by step, stay present in the moment, cultivate positive emotions, and engage in meaningful activities with your partner. These practices work hand in hand with the brain's neuroplasticity, allowing you to rewire your thinking patterns and reduce anxiety and overthinking. Remember, it takes dedication, patience, and support, but by breaking free from the anxiety thread loop, you can nurture healthier relationships and experience better emotional wellbeing.

WORKBOOK FOUR

Section 1: Understanding Your Anxiety

- What are some common triggers for anxiety and overthinking in your relationship?

- How does anxiety impact your thoughts, emotions, and behaviors in your relationship?

- Reflect on past experiences where anxiety and overthinking have affected your relationship(s). What patterns or themes do you notice?

Section 2: Cognitive Restructuring

- Identify one negative thought or belief you commonly have about yourself or your relationship. Challenge this belief by asking yourself: What evidence supports this thought? What evidence contradicts it?

- Replace negative thoughts with more balanced and helpful alternatives. Write down affirmations or positive statements you can repeat to yourself when anxiety arises.

- How can you reframe situations in your relationship to focus on more realistic and constructive perspectives?

Section 3: Graded Exposure

- Create a fear hierarchy related to your anxiety. List situations or actions that elicit that anxiety, starting from least to most anxiety-provoking.

- Choose one situation from your fear hierarchy and plan a small step you can take to expose yourself to it. What support or resources do you need to ensure a safe and manageable exposure?

- Reflect on your experiences after engaging in graded exposure. How did you feel before, during, and after the exposure? Did your anxiety and overthinking change? What did you learn from the process?

Section 4: Building Positive Experiences

- Identify activities or hobbies that bring you joy and fulfillment. How often do you engage in these activities? How can you incorporate them into your routine more regularly?

- Practice gratitude by reflecting on and writing down three things you appreciate about your relationship each day. How does this practice influence your mindset and overall wellbeing?

- Share positive experiences and moments of growth with your partner. How does celebrating these moments contribute to a stronger connection and reduced anxiety?

Section 6: Support and Self-Care

- Who can you turn to for support when you're feeling overwhelmed by anxiety and overthinking about your relationship? How can you communicate your needs effectively to them?

- What self-care practices are essential for managing your anxiety and promoting your wellbeing? Create a self-care plan and commit to implementing it regularly.

Remember, this workbook is designed to guide you through the process of loosening the anxiety thread loop. Take your time, be kind to yourself, and embrace the journey of growth and letting go. You have the strength and resilience to cultivate healthier, more fulfilling relationships.

CHAPTER FIVE

Deepening Your Connections

"The words of the reckless pierce like swords, but the tongue of the wise brings healing."

—Proverbs 12:18

"The most important thing in communication is hearing what isn't said."

—Peter Drucker

Malcolm had always believed that love is enough to keep a relationship going, which is why he didn't try to deepen his connection with Caroline when they got married— but it turns out he couldn't have been more wrong. As a kid, he was famed for being the cool, aloof kid who wasn't bothered by anything, but adulthood is a whole different ballgame, as he would soon come to know. Shortly after his marriage to Caroline, they began experiencing problems: he wouldn't make time to just relax and have a real conversation with her or sit on the couch with her and talk to her about things that matter (all of which build trust and intimacy in a relationship). Malcolm was as bullheaded as they come. Slowly, this led to misunderstandings which could have been resolved easily if the partners were communicating with each other. It then led to trust issues, which led to fights, and eventually a separation that left Malcolm wondering what went wrong.

So, tell me—what do you think went wrong? Hopefully, the answer is pretty clear: they didn't build a deep connection that would sustain and warm them during the cold, harsh times in life.

What does it mean to deepen your connection in a relationship? Just like it takes two to tango, it takes two partners to make the effort to be closer and more intimate with each other. Being deeply connected means being trusting and loving as well as supportive and communicating with each other about everything going on. These little "unimportant" things strengthen the bonds of a relationship and bring the partners closer as well as giving them a deeper understanding of each other.

The Role of Effective Communication

The role of effective communication in a relationship cannot be overemphasized (Smith, 2021). It is key to a healthy relationship. All couples have different modes of communication, so they have to find what works for them and stick to it. Communication helps us to understand our partner, which prevents major issues and deepens our connection (as long as we remain open and trusting enough to communicate). Communication is essential because no one is a superhuman with mind-reading powers; we actually have to say what's on our mind so we can work together with our partner to find solutions. The more we do this, the more each partner knows what the other needs, sometimes even without verbal communication.

Some of the reasons effective communication is so important are:

1. Intimacy: Intimacy can mean different things for different couples. For some, it's romantic; for some, it's the simple acts that make you feel like you are your partner's world. A simple act of intimacy could be bringing your partner who works as a teacher a cup of honey tea, knowing their voice is strained from work. These little things help show your partner that you listen to them when they talk about work or their life or the future. Effective communication is not just about talking but also about listening and trying to see things from their point of view, which gives you a deeper understanding of who they are and what makes them tick. When there is effective communication in your relationship, intimacy is a sure result.

2. Trust: Communicating your interests, thoughts, experiences, and ideas with your partner shows them you trust them and that they can trust you with the

same. This is a one-way ticket to a healthy relationship. Trust is one of the essential elements of a relationship. The presence of trust prevents unnecessary arguments that arise from assuming the worst of each other. When both partners trust each other completely, they have faith in each other, and whenever there's a problem, they can bring it up in a calm and respectful manner instead of casting blame without proof or interrogating each other because of their insecurity. When partners trust each other completely, they are emotionally connected and can weather any storm that may threaten their bond.

3. Companionship: Another important effect of communication is that it builds companionship. The sharing of interests and experiences creates a sense of comradeship between the partners, and having someone to whom you can talk about anything is the best treasure in the world.

4. Concentration on major problems: Another role of effective communication is that it helps partners focus on the major problems threatening their bond and allows them to make time to discuss and tackle these problems head-on, rather than avoiding them and getting distracted by little things.

Common Communication Pitfalls to Avoid

"He's a little scary but he's right. Let's talk."

"If you and your partner are struggling to understand one another's point of view, it's possible you may open yourself up to common communication mistakes" (Baum, 2021). Here are some common communication pitfalls to avoid:

1. Not listening: When having conversations with your partner, you should be giving them your full attention, and that means staying off your phone and turning off the music or television so you can focus. However, some people do all of this and still don't listen to their partner. Listening to your partner involves hearing what they're saying, giving them the floor to express themselves, and not interrupting them, but also asking questions to show you're interested and engaged.

Failing to listen and interrupting just to drop a rebuttal or two is rude and can lead to a whole myriad of problems, which could sink the relationship.

2. Not acknowledging your partner's point of view: Is there real communication between partners if they don't try to see things from each other's point of view? No, there isn't. Why? Because refusing to acknowledge your partner's point of view will make them feel like you don't care. Seeing things from their perspective will help you understand why they do things, why they need more assurance, why they react the way they do, etc.

3. Jumping to conclusions: Jumping to conclusions about what your partner is discussing with you because you feel you've heard something like it before or you know how it ends is just rude, but is also actually quite common. It's disastrous to constantly interrupt your partner and assume you know what they're going to say. By doing this, you're missing the message they're trying to convey and at the same time you're making them feel unimportant.

4. Avoiding conflict: Most people would rather avoid a difficult situation than tackle it head-on. Why? Because they would rather avoid conflict than face it due to the effects it might have on their relationship. The irony here is that avoiding conflict has a greater negative effect

on a relationship than facing such conflict. When partners are withholding information from each other or refusing to address problems, the relationship is sure to crumble sooner rather than later.

5. Being indirect and/or closed off: Communicating indirectly with your partner because you feel they should know what you're saying or what you want is not exactly clever. We need to understand that our partners cannot read our minds, so expecting them to know what we want when we don't express it is weird and disastrous for the relationship. There should be "no guesswork that opens you up to potential communication struggles" (Baum, 2021). Being straightforward with your partner helps prevent misunderstandings and larger problems.

The Art of Active Listening

I know you're probably thinking, "This is my thing; I'm a good listener." Well, I'm sorry to tell you that you're most likely not. Perhaps you've heard the quote, "There's a difference between listening and waiting for your turn to speak" (Grossman, 2018). There's a difference between actively listening to someone and just waiting for them to finish so you can drop your rebuttal or give a response. Many relationships have been crippled and destroyed because of the inability of the partners to actively listen to each other. When actively listening to someone, you're paying them the utmost attention, and this shows them how valuable they are to you. Active listening is an art, and like every piece of artwork, it takes time and effort to create something beautiful (which, in this case, is a healthy, long-lasting relationship).

The following are tips to help you become a better active listener:

1. Focus and pay rapt attention to the speaker: To actively listen to someone, you have to pay full attention to them and what they're talking about. Don't have your phone in your hand; put it, and any other distractions, away (Grossman, 2018). You must make eye contact in order to catch their facial expressions and deduce how they're feeling as well as read their body language and tone. All these factors will give you an idea of how they're truly feeling and the message they're trying to pass across to you. Some individuals say one thing and mean the other, so it's the attention to minor details that prevents misunderstandings and costly misinterpretations.

2. No interruptions: Being an active listener means more than just hearing what your partner has to say; it means not interrupting them even when they say something you don't agree with. Interruptions don't necessarily have to be verbal, either—you could interrupt your

partner by fake coughing or making obscene gestures. The absence of interruptions in your conversations will make your partner feel valued and loved.

3. Ask clarifying questions: If you don't understand something, asking questions like, "Can you explain that more?" when your partner pauses is key to being an active listener. It shows that you're interested in the conversation at hand, that you genuinely care, and that you want to know more.

4. Don't jump to conclusions: There's a reason this was also included in our list of communication pitfalls in the previous section. When you're listening to someone, it's critical not to jump to conclusions. All of us sometimes battle with the urge to jump in and end a statement for someone or guess quite loudly how a story ends. However, this behavior can be quite disastrous for a relationship, as it is disrespectful and not part of active listening.

Other quick tips include:

- Don't impose your own opinions.
- Don't get defensive and emotional.
- Don't be judgmental.

Building Deeper Connections With Vulnerability

What does vulnerability have to do with it? Well, vulnerability is "a big part of authenticity and connection" (Iyarn, 2020). However, in today's world, vulnerability is synonymous with weakness, and to be weak means to be trampled upon by others. This is why many hide their real selves and pretend to be emotionless and cold. An example of how society has made us believe vulnerability is weak is the saying, "Men don't cry." Instead of being encouraged to express their emotions and talk about problems with someone, men are taught to "suck it up" and "man up." But what many don't know is that being vulnerable with someone shows them the real you—and by the real you, I don't mean the detached version of you, but the corny, goofy, and emotional hot mess we all are inside. Being vulnerable and expressing your emotions doesn't make you weak; it shows that you're strong and confident enough to be open about yourself.

Being vulnerable with someone builds intimacy and stronger connections, which is key to a healthy, happy relationship. When we show someone our most vulnerable self, it sends a message that we trust them, and this builds a deep connection that can weather any storm. It also creates a safe space for them to open up to you in return. Being vulnerable with someone shows them your flaws and insecurities; it reveals your imperfect and beautiful self, and this is a step towards building a relationship that will stand the test of time. Vulnerability can also lead to growth as we accept that we're not going to be perfect no matter how hard we try, but we can be the best versions of our flawed selves if we try hard enough.

Being vulnerable builds deeper and more meaningful connections and gives us the chance to be open and experience ourselves in ways we haven't dreamed of. The first step to being vulnerable is accepting that you're imperfect and beautiful just as you are, then working towards mastering your imperfections. With time, you'll become the best version of yourself.

The Role of Intimacy

Intimacy, though hard to define, is that unexplainable feeling of trust and closeness you have with your partner. It is that feeling you get when you're sitting together in silence, holding hands. Sometimes you don't even have to speak to understand what the other the person is currently feeling. Intimacy "is all about feeling alive, content, ecstatic, and at the same time, being vulnerable" (Smith, 2021).

Emotional, intellectual, spiritual, and physical intimacy are all aspects of intimacy. Emotionally speaking, sharing your feelings, concerns, dreams, and weaknesses with your partner creates a secure and supportive environment for real self-expression. Intellectual intimacy involves having meaningful talks, sharing ideas, and respecting one another's point of view. Spiritual intimacy brings you together on a deeper level, allowing you to share your values, beliefs, and purpose. It involves being able to pray with and for each other, growing together as you both learn from the Word, and work together in fulfilling purpose and enriching your lives.

Intimacy is essential for the growth and deepening of your relationship. It entails a strong emotional, physical, and psychological bond with your partner, promoting feelings of closeness, vulnerability, and trust. Anxiety and overthinking, unfortunately, frequently obstruct one's ability to completely feel and grow in intimacy.

Anxiety and overthinking can impede the formation and maintenance of intimacy in a variety of ways. First, anxiety is frequently caused by a fear of vulnerability and rejection. We may hesitate to open up emotionally or disclose our actual selves when we are apprehensive, fearing criticism or desertion. Overthinking can increase our worries by causing us to overthink every interaction, mistrust our partner's motives, or invent scenarios that may not be accurate. These behaviors can obstruct intimacy by keeping us from truly engaging and connecting with our partner.

Intimacy is a wonderful and transformational journey that involves transparency, vulnerability, and a real desire to connect with your partner. Here are some suggestions for cultivating intimacy:

1. Create a safe space: Create a non-judgmental setting in which you and your partner may express yourselves genuinely. Encourage open conversation, active listening, and respect for one another. This secure environment will promote closeness and trust.

2. Demonstrate emotional availability: Be emotionally accessible to your partner and receptive to their feelings and experiences. Demonstrate empathy, understanding, and support. Allow your partner to connect with your inner self by openly and honestly communicating your own thoughts and feelings. Remember, intimacy requires vulnerability. Even if it's difficult, keep reminding yourself that there is strength in vulnerability and give yourself to your partner. You can also discuss the difficulties you have opening up, and together you can work on a solution or compromise that works for you both. Doing this should make you less scared of judgment or of being hurt.

3. Spend quality time together: Schedule uninterrupted time to interact with your partner. Engage in intimate activities such as going on dates, taking walks together, or simply having meaningful conversations. Take a break from serious activities once in a while and just have fun together. Do silly things like having a food fight, or playing board games and attaching prizes.

Quality time establishes the foundation for emotional intimacy.

4. Explore shared interests: Participate in things that both of you enjoy and find meaningful. Discover new activities or rediscover old ones together. Shared interests and experiences strengthen bonds and provide for quality time and shared memories.

5. Practice trust and honesty: The cornerstone of intimacy is trust. Maintain open and honest communication and be trustworthy. Trust your partner and be open and vulnerable with them. Building trust lays a solid basis for intimacy to flourish.

6. Pursue continual growth: Intimacy is a lifelong adventure that requires continual growth. Be willing to learn new things about yourself and your relationship. Accept new experiences, challenges, and opportunities for personal development. Allow your relationship to deepen and evolve through time.

Humor Also Helps

Have you ever heard the phrase, "Laughter is the best medicine"? Not only is laughter good for you, but having a sense of humor can be attractive to your partner as well (Greengross, 2018). In fact, a sense of humor often shows up near the top of people's list of desirable traits in a romantic partner (DiDenato, 2013).

Humor, while often overlooked, can play an important role in deepening your connection and promoting a sense of joy and closeness in your relationship. It has the ability to relieve stress, reduce anxiety, and generate a happy and lighthearted environment. You may find you can let go of some fear and overthinking by embracing humor, allowing for a more honest and meaningful connection with your partner.

Here are just a few of the benefits of bringing humor into your relationship:

1. Icebreaker and bonding tool: Humor is an excellent icebreaker, allowing people to feel more at ease with one another. Sharing a chuckle or a funny moment might assist in breaking down boundaries and fostering togetherness. It can be a terrific approach to start a conversation, connect with someone, and establish trust.

2. Stress reduction: Relationships can be stressful, conflicting, and challenging at times. By brightening the mood and dissipating tension, humor functions as a natural stress reliever. It provides a brief respite from the stresses of everyday life, allowing you and your partner to rest, recharge, and approach challenges with new eyes.

3. Enhanced communication: Humor can improve communication by creating a lively and open environment. It promotes active listening by allowing you and your partner to engage in clever banter, share amusing anecdotes, and laugh together. This lighthearted way to communicate fosters greater understanding, empathy, and a stronger bond between partners.

Clearly, humor in your everyday life and in your relationship can be a wonderful and gratifying experience. Here are some tips for incorporating humor into your interactions with your partner:

1. Be playful: Approach situations with a lighthearted attitude. Look for ways to add humor into regular activities, such as lively banter, witty quips, or amusing observations. Allow your imagination to run wild (not too wild, though!) and embrace your inner child.

2. Find common ground: Discover mutual hobbies and humor preferences with your partner. Together, you can watch comedy shows or movies, or read funny books. Discuss hilarious anecdotes or funny memories from your past. Developing a shared sense of humor strengthens your bond.

3. Embrace mistakes and laughter: Instead of being frustrated by errors or mishaps, learn to laugh at them. Find humor in life's imperfections and motivate your partner to do the same. Laughing together improves your bond and boosts resilience.

Keep in mind that comedy is very subjective, and what one person considers hilarious may not be entertaining to another. There is a difference between laughing at someone and laughing with them. So, even when having fun, be cautious and sensitive. Genuine humor should provide joy and connection.

Conflict Resolution Strategies You Need

"Conflict is inherently uncomfortable for most of us, in both personal and professional contexts, but learning to effectively handle conflicts in a productive, healthy way is essential" (Krakoff, n.d). Conflicts "are struggles that can arise during an active disagreement of opinions or interests, so it's important to understand how to navigate and resolve them" (Herrity, 2022). Developing the skill of conflict resolution can take many years of practice and effort, but there are some simple things you can start out with to begin improving this skill (Krakoff, n.d).

Any relationship will inevitably have conflict, but how we handle those conflicts has a big influence on just how strong and deep our bonds are. And so, it is important that we develop effective conflict resolution techniques. Here are some crucial tactics to take into account:

1. Open and respectful communication: Conflict resolution requires effective communication. Establish a private, judgment-free area where both of you feel free to communicate your ideas and emotions. Engage in active listening, make an effort to comprehend one another's viewpoints, and react with respect and empathy.

2. Focus on the issue, not your partner: When discussing the conflict, remember to keep the conversation on the specific issue at hand rather than insulting, criticizing, or demeaning your partner and what they have to say. Keep your focus on finding a solution rather than bringing up sensitive personal topics (such as past disagreements you have had, or the past mistakes of your partner) that could worsen the problem and prevent you both from communicating effectively. You can do this by taking a deep breath or a timeout whenever you notice you are both off-topic. Waiting for your emotions to cool off is also an effective tip; however, be careful it does not reach the point of keeping malice.

3. Engage in problem-solving: Use your disagreements as a chance to work together on a resolution through

cooperative problem-solving. Take into account all of your options and seek solutions that satisfy the requirements of both of you. Be adaptable and open-minded, prepared to consider your partner's opinions and thoughts.

4. Use "I" not "you": Use "I" phrases to convey your thoughts and feelings to avoid placing blame or coming across as defensive. For example, say, "I feel hurt when…" rather than, "You always…" This way, you are taking accountability rather than blaming your partner and causing them to lash out in defense .

5. Apologize and forgive: If you have offended your partner or made a mistake, accept responsibility for your actions and provide a heartfelt apology. Likewise, be willing to overlook your partner's transgressions and let go of grudges. Forgiveness and apologies are effective means of mending your relationship and strengthening your bond.

Keep in mind that conflict resolution is a continuous process that calls for patience, understanding, and a sincere desire to maintain and nurture the relationship. By using these techniques, you may improve your relationship and let go of any anxiety or overthinking that could result from unresolved problems.*

* **Scan this QR Code** and limit the unresolved problems by discovering how to deal with difficult people. This second eBook BONUS *"How to Deal with Difficult People"* will help you.

Setting and Maintaining Healthy Boundaries

You may think that boundaries are only for people you're not very close with or who consistently try to hurt or offend you in some way, but they're actually necessary in romantic relationships too. In your relationship, you can "think of [boundaries] as a framework rather than rigid guidelines" (Pattemore, 2021). Setting and upholding healthy boundaries is essential for developing and fostering long-lasting, satisfying bonds. Boundaries are rules we set up to safeguard our physical, emotional, and mental health while also honoring the boundaries of others. We build a foundation of trust, encourage self-care, and lessen anxiety and overthinking by establishing and upholding boundaries.

"Without healthy boundaries, your relationships can become toxic and unsatisfying and your well-being can suffer" (Reid, 2023). Our boundaries indicate where we stop and others start. They aid in the development of our sense of self, independence, and private space. Boundaries cover a wide range of topics, including time-related, emotional, physical, and intellectual ones. Setting and upholding boundaries begin with understanding their significance.

Here are some helpful hints to help you with establishing and maintaining healthy boundaries with your partner:

1. Begin with self-reflection: Take some time to consider your own needs, values, and personal boundaries. Consider what makes you feel at ease and what makes you uncomfortable. Understanding your personal limits is vital before conveying them effectively to your partner.

2. Engage in open communication: Discuss your boundaries with your partner in an open and honest manner. Express your needs, desires, and expectations clearly while carefully listening to their point of view. Try to talk gently but firmly as much as possible. You might even try to find the humor in the issue and joke about it once the serious talk is finished; this can soothe whatever sting your partner may have felt throughout the discussion.

3. Be specific and concrete: When establishing boundaries, be specific and provide concrete examples. Define which behaviors, activities, or situations are acceptable and which are not. This clarity helps to avoid

misunderstandings and keeps you both on the same page.

4. Listen to your gut: When it comes to boundaries, pay heed to your feelings and trust your gut. Respect your intuition if something doesn't seem right or correspond with your values and principles. Trust yourself and explain your feelings to your significant other honestly.

5. Have mutual respect: Boundaries should be mutually respected. Respect your partner's boundaries as much as they should respect yours. This reciprocal respect generates an environment of understanding and equality in the relationship.

6. Do regular check-ins: Reevaluate your boundaries by regularly checking in with yourself and your partner. Boundaries may need to change or evolve as your relationship does. Continuous conversation and good boundary maintenance are made possible through open and honest communication.

Keep in mind that boundaries are an important part of both self-care and a healthy relationship, and that it's acceptable to alter your boundaries as you grow and develop and gain experience.

Effective Communication Worksheets for Couples

Instructions: Answer the following questions and complete the suggested exercises to improve your communication with your partner.

Part 1: Self-Reflection

- How would you rate your current communication skills with your partner on a scale of 1 to 10? (1 = poor, 10 = excellent) Why did you choose this rating?

- Identify one area of communication that you would like to improve in your relationship. Describe why this area is important to you.

- What are some barriers or challenges that you and your partner face when it comes to effective communication?

Part 2: Active Listening

- Describe what active listening means to you and why it is crucial for effective communication in a relationship.

- Recall a recent conversation with your partner where your active listening was lacking. What could you have done differently to improve your listening skills in that situation?

Exercise:

Choose a topic of discussion with your partner. Take turns speaking and practicing active listening skills. Afterward, reflect on the experience and discuss how it felt to be listened to attentively.

Part 3: Non-Verbal Communication

- How important is non-verbal communication in your relationship? Provide some examples of non-verbal cues that you and your partner commonly use.

- Reflect on a recent disagreement or conflict with your partner. Were there any non-verbal cues that were misinterpreted or that contributed to the misunderstanding? How could you address this in the future?

Exercise:

Engage in a role-play activity with your partner where you communicate without using words. Pay attention to each other's non-verbal cues and discuss the challenges and insights gained from this exercise.

Part 4: Expressing Needs and Emotions

- Why is it important to effectively express your needs and emotions to your partner? What impact can it have on your relationship?

- Share one specific need or emotion that you find challenging to express to your partner. What makes it difficult, and how do you think it affects your relationship?

Exercise:

Write a letter or journal entry expressing your needs or emotions to your partner. Take turns sharing and discussing the contents of your letters, focusing on understanding and support.

Part 5: Conflict Resolution

- Describe a conflict resolution style that you and your partner often adopt. How effective is this style in resolving conflicts? What improvements could be made?

- Think of a recent conflict that escalated and was not resolved satisfactorily. How could you have approached the situation differently to achieve a more positive outcome?

Exercise:

Choose a previous conflict that remains unresolved. Practice using active listening, expressing needs, and finding a compromise or resolution together. Reflect on the process and its impact on your relationship.

Conclusion:

Improving communication skills takes time and practice. Use this worksheet as a starting point for open discussions with your partner. Remember, effective communication is essential for building a strong and healthy relationship.

Vulnerability and Intimacy Exercises

As we discussed in the section on vulnerability, "vulnerability creates true, meaningful connection" (Mantell, n.d). If you can create vulnerability and intimacy within your relationship, "you share your feelings, needs, fears, successes, and failures knowing you will continue to be loved and cared for by your partner" (Madison, 2020). And although it might be extremely scary, vulnerability is interwoven with intimacy, and one cannot exist without the other.

Here are some exercises you can practice:

1. Show gratitude: Express your gratitude for and to each other. Tell your partner about specific qualities you value in them or positive parts of your connection. This

activity encourages emotional intimacy and vulnerability and cultivates a positive mindset.

2. Write love letters: Express your affection, awe, and gratitude through sincere letters to one another. Spend some time thinking about how you feel about your partner. Share these letters together, letting yourself be open to receiving love and encouragement.

3. Schedule emotional check-ins: Continually update one another on your emotional health. Open-ended inquiries like, "How are you feeling today?" and, "Is there anything on your mind that you'd like to share?" are appropriate. This fosters vulnerability by giving each of you the chance to express more intense feelings and worries.

4. Share weaknesses: Talk to your partner about any anxieties or weaknesses you may have. Talk about your aspirations, worries, and insecurities. This activity fosters closeness and trust by providing a safe area for both partners to comfort and reassure one another.

5. Build trust: Take part in trust-building activities that call for transparency and require you to rely on one another. This can be trust falls, blindfolded trust walks, or other activities that foster a sense of security and strengthen your bonds of affection.

Remember that vulnerability exercises should be approached with sensitivity and respect for each other's comfort levels. It's important to create an environment where both of you will feel safe and supported. There is bound to be some discomfort or fear, as vulnerability and intimacy can be scary to some; however, since these exercises are to foster intimacy, you should try as much as possible to ignore your fears and allow yourself to be vulnerable.

MAIN IDEAS

Think back to Malcolm's situation. In the wake of his separation from his wife, Caroline, Malcolm underwent a period of self-reflection and soul-searching. He realized that his belief in the power of love alone was misguided, and that sustaining a healthy relationship requires active effort and a willingness to deepen emotional connections. Through this painful experience, Malcolm learned the importance of effective communication, vulnerability, and being present for his partner. He vowed to make changes in his approach to his relationship, committing to being more attentive, empathetic, and open. He and Caroline eventually got back together—but not after a lot of hard work, patience, and soul-baring exercises and questions.

Deepening your connection with your partner is a wonderful journey that can assist you in letting go of anxiety and overthinking in your relationship. By practicing self-awareness, embracing vulnerability, and employing effective strategies such as effective communication, setting healthy boundaries, humor, and engaging in intimacy exercises, we can create a solid foundation for a meaningful and fulfilling relationship. It is through these practices that we can cultivate trust, intimacy, and emotional connection, ultimately allowing us to experience deeper levels of love and fulfillment in our relationship.

WORKBOOK FIVE

Section 1: Understanding Anxiety and Overthinking in Your Relationship

1.1 Reflective Questions:

- How do anxiety and overthinking impact your relationships?

- What are the common triggers or situations that provoke anxiety or overthinking for you?

- How do anxiety and overthinking affect your ability to connect with your partner?

1.2 Exercise: Identifying Anxiety and Overthinking Patterns

- Keep a journal of your anxious thoughts and overthinking episodes in your relationship.

- Reflect on the underlying fears, doubts, or insecurities that drive these patterns.

- Identify any recurring themes or patterns that emerge from your observations.

Section 2: Effective Communication for Deeper Connections

2.1 Reflective Questions:

- How do you currently communicate with your partner during challenging or emotional moments?

- What barriers or obstacles do you face when trying to express your needs and emotions?

- How can you improve your communication to foster a deeper emotional connection?

2.2 Exercise: Active Listening and Empathy

- Practice active listening skills by fully focusing on your partner's words, non-verbal cues, and emotions.

- Reflect on your partner's perspective and validate their feelings.

- Engage in empathy exercises to better understand and connect with your partner's experiences.

Section 3: Cultivating Emotional Connection

3.1 Reflective Questions:

- How would you describe the current level of emotional connection in your relationship?

- What activities or experiences deepen your emotional connection with your partner?

- Are there any barriers preventing you from cultivating a deeper emotional connection?

3.2 Exercise: Quality Time and Shared Experiences

- Set aside dedicated quality time with your partner, free from distractions and technology.

- Engage in activities that promote shared experiences and emotional connection, such as going on dates, taking walks, or pursuing mutual interests.

- Reflect on the impact of these activities on your emotional connection and discuss with your partner.

CHAPTER SIX

Building Healthy Habits

"Above all else, guard your heart, for everything you do flows from it."

—Proverbs 4:23

"A healthy relationship keeps the doors and windows wide open. Plenty of air is circulating and no one feels trapped. Relationships thrive in this environment. Keep your doors and windows open. If the person is meant to be in your life, all the open doors and windows in the world will not make them leave. Trust the truth."

—Anonymous.

Hailey and Justin's relationship blossomed amidst the vibrant backdrop of a bustling city. Drawn to each other's charismatic personalities and shared interests, they embarked on a passionate romance. However, beneath the surface, their bond was marred by a lack of trust and mutual respect.

As time passed, insecurities took hold. They engaged in a destructive cycle of mind games, testing the limits of each other's loyalty and commitment. Communication became a minefield filled with passive-aggressive remarks and suppressed emotions.

Their toxic dynamic eroded the foundation of their love, leaving them emotionally drained and disconnected.

Navigating the intricacies of love while tackling life's challenges can be quite the balancing act. Falling in love might be a walk in the park, but keeping that flame burning amidst the daily grind requires some effort.

For those with an inclination to overthink and a touch of anxiety, prioritizing their relationship can feel like a daunting task. Balancing work pressures, financial responsibilities, parenting duties, and an ever-growing to-do list can amplify their worries, making it harder to be fully present for their partner. The constant cycle of thoughts and analysis can become overwhelming, leaving little room to nurture the relationship amidst the chaos of everyday life.

However, recognizing the impact of anxiety and overthinking is the first step towards finding a healthier equilibrium. By acknowledging these challenges and taking proactive steps, like practicing self-care and open communication, individuals can create space for their relationship to thrive. It's about finding that delicate balance between addressing life's demands and cherishing the emotional bond that brought you and your partner together.

Remember, love doesn't have to be perfect, but it's the little moments of togetherness that make it all worthwhile.

Why Your Relationship Needs Healthy Habits

Maintaining healthy habits while in a relationship can contribute significantly to one's happiness and life satisfaction. Those with healthy habits are less prone to encountering physical and mental health issues. Extensive research has explored and revealed the numerous benefits that healthy relationships can have on our overall wellbeing, encompassing both our habits and our mental health.

Let us further explore the profound positive impacts that cultivating healthy habits in your relationship can bring to your lives.

1. Decreased stress: "Having someone to talk to, rely on, and share the load can have a significant impact on how we perceive the problem" (Smith, 2021). The act of sharing our thoughts, concerns, and burdens with another person can provide us with emotional support, a fresh perspective, and a sense of shared responsibility. It is vital to nurture a meaningful connection with your partner, as they can greatly contribute to your overall wellbeing and resilience in the face of life's challenges.

2. Added meaning to life: A healthy relationship "can give a person a sense of purpose and fulfillment" (Acenda Integrated Health, n.d.). Knowing that you are

genuinely loved and cared for by another person can infuse your life with a sense of purpose and meaning due to the support, progress, and shared dreams that partners foster together in a romantic relationship. Being in a loving relationship helps people to support each other's dreams and work together to achieve common goals. As both partners contribute to each other's personal development and journey, this combined effort fosters a strong sense of unity and shared purpose.

3. Encouragement of healthy behaviors: If you're in a loving relationship, it's likely that your partner "encourage[s] [you] to exercise, eat healthy, and follow up with medical problems" (Phelps, 2020). They often serve as a source of encouragement and support, motivating us to prioritize our physical and mental wellbeing. Whether it's through gentle reminders, joint participation in activities, or offering guidance, our romantic partner can encourage us to exercise regularly, make healthier food choices, and address medical issues quickly.

4. Increased happiness: It's true; being in a healthy relationship can actually make you happier (Salaky, 2017). A healthy relationship provides a strong emotional foundation. It offers a safe space to express

your emotions, share your joys and sorrows, and feel understood and validated. Having a supportive partner who listens, empathizes, and offers comfort can significantly enhance your emotional wellbeing and overall happiness.

5. Enhanced communication: By actively listening, expressing thoughts and emotions clearly, and resolving conflicts constructively, you can improve your understanding of each other, minimize misunderstandings, and foster a deeper connection.

6. Increased trust and intimacy: When partners consistently prioritize their wellbeing and maintain healthy habits, it establishes a sense of reliability and trust. They can rely on each other to prioritize their health and make choices that support their overall wellbeing, which strengthens the foundation of trust in the relationship.

A Happy Couple Is a Healthy Couple

"We're pretty good at this when we work together."

When we think of a happy couple, certain individuals we know may come to mind. These couples are often characterized by their visible happiness and inseparable bond. We observe the genuine smiles exchanged between the wife and husband, as well as their constant laughter and playful interactions. The wife's affectionate way of speaking to her husband and the husband's gestures of physical closeness, like placing his arm around her or resting his hand on her back, leave a lasting impression.

In the presence of such couples, we can sense the sparkle in their eyes and witness the effortless way they engage with each other. Stepping into their home, we immediately notice the absence of tension and the abundance of comfort and tranquility.

Those couples who exude happiness and love seem to possess a secret or knowledge that eludes us. It's as if they have discovered a transformative key that could potentially revive even the most lackluster or damaged relationships.

So, what does a happy couple look like specifically?

1. They are happy individuals: And by happiness, we don't mean "superficial emotions" (Los Angeles Christian Counseling, 2020). The Bible tells us that "*a happy heart is good medicine and a joyful mind causes healing, but a broken heart dries up the bones*" (Proverbs 17:22). In relationships, true happiness involves emotional wellbeing, compatibility, effective communication, mutual support, quality time, and intimacy. When these aspects are nurtured, they contribute to a deeper sense of fulfillment and satisfaction within the partnership. True happiness in relationships encompasses a lasting and genuine sense of joy and contentment.

2. They have fun together: Happy couples find joy in spending time together and prioritize having fun in their relationship. They actively seek out activities and experiences that bring them pleasure and create positive memories. By engaging in shared interests, exploring new adventures, or simply enjoying each other's company, they create a vibrant and enjoyable dynamic.

3. They pray together: Prayer increases marital satisfaction and decreases the chances of infidelity (Los Angeles Christian Counseling, 2020). 1 Thessalonians 5:16-18 says, "*Rejoice always, pray without ceasing, give thanks in all circumstances; for this is the will of God in Christ Jesus for you.*" These practices of rejoicing, praying, and giving thanks together create a foundation of positivity, spirituality, and appreciation, enhancing the happiness and fulfillment a couple finds in their relationship.

4. They forgive easily: The ability to forgive easily is a key characteristic that contributes to a happy couple's overall wellbeing and relationship satisfaction. Forgiveness allows partners to let go of past hurts, conflicts, and mistakes, promoting emotional healing and growth within the relationship. By forgiving easily, couples create a climate of understanding, empathy, and compassion, fostering a sense of trust and emotional safety. It prevents the accumulation of negative emotions and resentment, allowing the couple to move forward and maintain a positive and harmonious connection. This willingness to forgive promotes effective communication, conflict resolution, and the ability to work through challenges together.

5. They don't forget the things that initially drew them together: It is common for happy couples to hold on to

the memories and qualities that initially attracted them to each other. They cherish and remember the things that brought them together and sparked their connection. This includes the shared interests, values, and experiences that formed the foundation of their relationship. By not forgetting these initial aspects, happy couples keep their bond strong and maintain a sense of appreciation for one another. They actively nurture and celebrate the qualities and moments that made them fall in love. This practice helps to sustain their positive feelings and attraction, allowing the relationship to thrive over time. By holding on to the essence of what drew them together, happy couples continue to find joy, fulfillment, and a deep sense of connection in their partnership.

Setting Smart Goals for Your Relationship

Relationship goals serve as a guiding mission statement for couples, tailored to their unique dynamic. They can range in complexity, depending on the preferences of each couple. The essence of a well-crafted relationship goal lies in its ability to align with the core values of both partners. Furthermore, these goals should possess a quality of flexibility and adaptability, enabling them to evolve alongside the changing stages of the partners' lives. These smart goals include, but are not limited to:

1. Financial independence: When working on financial independence as a couple, you can establish smart goals such as saving a specific amount of money each month, creating a joint budget, reducing unnecessary expenses, or seeking additional sources of income. By setting these goals, you can approach your financial journey with clarity, focus, and a higher chance of success.

2. Making time for each other: You don't necessarily have to schedule one-on-one time in your calendar, but you should spend time together that doesn't involve being on your phones (Davis, 2022). If you're aiming for a satisfying relationship, it's crucial to make quality time a top priority. Taking the time to connect and bond with your partner is essential for nurturing your emotional connection. Whether it's going on dates, enjoying hobbies together, or simply having meaningful conversations, allocating quality time is a fundamental aspect of building a happy and healthy relationship.

3. Gratitude: Another important goal within your relationship should be expressing gratitude. This is all about recognizing and appreciating your partner's efforts, qualities, and actions. By actively showing gratitude, you can create a positive and supportive atmosphere in your relationship. Express appreciation

for both the big and small gestures, acknowledge each other's contributions, and regularly say thank you. Gratitude reinforces a sense of value, love, and respect in your relationship. When you make a conscious effort to show gratitude, you strengthen your bond and cultivate a more fulfilling and harmonious partnership.

4. "Me" time: Making room for personal solitude is essential in any relationship. You should intentionally set aside periods where each of you can have uninterrupted alone time. This goal recognizes the importance of individuality and self-care within your partnership. By dedicating specific moments to personal solitude, you create space for self-reflection, relaxation, and pursuing individual interests. This time allows each partner to recharge, rejuvenate, and maintain a healthy sense of self. It also fosters personal growth, independence, and self-awareness, which all contribute to a stronger and more balanced relationship.

5. Maintaining a healthy lifestyle: Setting up healthy eating and exercise habits as you age is important, and having a partner who shares the same goals can really help you stick with your health commitments (Davis, 2022). This helps to improve the health and wellbeing of both you and your partner.

Introducing New Routines

We all have habits that become ingrained in our daily routine, such as brushing our teeth, making the bed, or unwinding with a drink after a long day. These activities become second nature as we perform them without much thought.

When it comes to relationships, routines are often associated with mundane tasks necessary for a smoothly functioning life. However, routines can be more than that. They can serve as valuable tools in maintaining a strong and stable relationship, especially during stressful or transitional periods.

Positive rituals within a relationship can offer significant benefits. They have the power to enhance communication and connection between partners, leading to a greater sense of security and reducing any doubts or uncertainties that may arise.

These rituals can be simple acts of love and affection, such as sharing a daily hug, having a regular date night, or exchanging notes of appreciation. By incorporating these rituals into the relationship, you can strengthen your bond as a couple and navigate challenges more effectively.

Healthy Habits to Prioritize in Your Relationship

While no relationship is without its challenges, it is evident that some couples thrive while others struggle. So, what sets them apart? The reality is that happiness in a relationship is not a matter of chance. In fact, the healthiest and happiest couples are intentional in their efforts to build and sustain their love.

The healthy habits to prioritize are:

1. Making your spiritual wellbeing a priority: Prioritizing spiritual wellbeing in your relationship includes praying together, going to church and worship concerts together, and studying the Word together (Walters, 2022). As a couple, prioritizing your spiritual wellbeing involves jointly nurturing and cultivating your spiritual connection and growth.

2. Communicating: By now, we are pretty familiar with the idea that communication is key for a healthy relationship (Hall, 2020). It involves the ability to convey thoughts, feelings, and needs clearly and to actively listen to one another. It also allows partners to understand each other on a deeper level. For more specific tips, you can revisit Chapter 5.

3. Asking rather than assuming: In any relationship, one crucial habit to prioritize is avoiding assumptions and instead practicing open communication by asking questions. Assuming can lead to misunderstandings, misinterpretations, and unnecessary conflicts. By taking the time to ask questions (asking gently and politely, not interrogating like a drill sergeant) and seek

clarification, you create an atmosphere of understanding, empathy, and trust.

4. Sharing household responsibilities: This entails actively participating in the various tasks and chores required to maintain a functional and comfortable living environment. By sharing these responsibilities, couples foster a sense of teamwork, equality, and mutual support. It helps prevent feelings of burden or resentment that can arise when one person feels overwhelmed with all the household duties.

This also promotes fairness and balance in the relationship, as both partners contribute their time and effort to maintain the home they share. Moreover, it allows for better time management and reduces individual stress levels, freeing up quality time to spend together or pursue personal interests. Effective communication and cooperation are key to successfully sharing household responsibilities, ensuring that you both feel heard, understood, and valued. By prioritizing this habit, you can create a harmonious and supportive environment where the workload is shared, leading to a stronger and more balanced relationship.

5. Trusting each other: Trust is a fundamental habit to prioritize in your relationship. It serves as the cornerstone for a strong and healthy connection. Trust

is built on honesty, integrity, and reliability. It means having confidence in your partner's character and intentions. Prioritizing trust entails open and honest communication in which both partners feel free to share their opinions and emotions. It also includes honoring commitments and being reliable. Building trust takes time and consistency to demonstrate dependability and commitment.

Practicing Gratitude and Affection

Expressing gratitude and affection to your partner offers numerous benefits. However, consistently finding meaningful ways to do so might be challenging. To help you cultivate gratitude and affection in your relationship, here are some helpful tips.

1. Give compliments: "Have you ever caught yourself thinking something nice about your partner, such as admiring the way they look, or how they interact with you and others? Instead of keeping that thought to yourself, say it out loud" (Howard, 2021). Take a moment to specifically acknowledge and communicate what you appreciated in that particular moment.

2. Express appreciation via notes, texts, or letters: Another way to show gratitude to your partner is by writing a heartfelt note, text, or letter. Taking the time to put

your thoughts into writing allows you to convey your feelings in a sincere and lasting way.

3. Pitch in and give your partner a break: An additional way to show gratitude to your partner is by offering to help and giving them a break. Take initiative in sharing responsibilities and tasks, allowing your partner some much-needed rest or time for themselves. This act of support and consideration demonstrates your appreciation for their efforts and can strengthen your bond.

Physical Activity Together

Engaging in physical activity has a direct influence on our mood, which in turn affects various aspects of our lives, including our relationships. Therefore, it is logical to believe that exercising together can strengthen your bond with your partner.

Physical activities as a couple provide a unique and shared experience. There are several ways to include fitness in your daily routine, whether you prefer to go for walks, bike rides, or hikes, or go swimming together.

Exercising together not only provides physical stimulation, but it also helps to bolster mental wellbeing. Working out with someone else provides mutual support and motivation, fostering a sense of solidarity and teamwork. Furthermore, physical exercise produces endorphins in the brain, which are natural mood-enhancing substances that can aid in reducing depression and stress. Here are a few more reasons why engaging in physical activity can improve your relationship:

1. Support and encouragement: Exercising together allows you to support and encourage each other, creating a positive and motivating environment.

2. Quality time: Engaging in physical activities provides dedicated time for you and your partner to bond and connect on a deeper level, strengthening your relationship.

3. Health benefits: Regular exercise has several health advantages, including greater fitness, improved cardiovascular health, increased energy levels, and general wellbeing, which can benefit both you and your partner.

4. Enhanced mood: Endorphins are released during physical exercise, which enhance mood and generate a sensation of enjoyment and fulfillment.

Forgiveness Is Key

You've probably heard about how important forgiveness is when it comes to relationships. Why? Well, "let's face it, people are not perfect" (Firestone, 2020). Finding a soulmate doesn't erase our individual differences, and sooner or later every couple is bound to have disagreements and points of contention. Striving to find a "perfect" partner will definitely lead to continuous disappointment. We all have a past and have done things we're not proud of. Rather than trying to do what only the blood of Jesus can do (washing others of their sins), we should accept our partner's different opinions, shortcomings, and flaws while cultivating forgiveness for a lasting relationship.

Forgiveness Worksheets

Reflection on Forgiveness:

a. Reflect on a recent situation where you felt hurt or wronged by your partner. What emotions did it evoke in you?

b. How did you respond to the situation? Did you express your feelings to your partner or hold them back?

c. How did the unresolved issue impact your relationship? Did it create distance, tension, or resentment?

d. Did you keep malice? Did you do something that you felt your partner deserved for hurting you?

Understanding the Importance of Forgiveness:

a. What does forgiveness mean to you in the context of your relationship?

b. Why do you think forgiveness is important for building a healthy and strong relationship?

c. How can practicing forgiveness positively impact both you and your partner?

d. What does the Bible say about forgiveness?

Communication and Empathy:

a. Have an open and honest conversation with your partner about forgiveness. Share your reflections from the previous exercises and ask for their perspective.

b. How does your partner perceive forgiveness? Are there any differences or similarities in your understanding?

c. How can you enhance your communication and empathy when discussing forgiveness in your relationship?

Setting Forgiveness Goals:

a. Identify specific situations or patterns where forgiveness is needed in your relationship.

b. Discuss and establish guidelines for expressing remorse and seeking forgiveness when one of you has caused hurt or harm.

c. What steps can you both take to foster forgiveness (such as active listening, empathetic understanding, and offering sincere apologies)?

d. Turn to God. Pray together with your partner on the issue of forgiveness. Search for Bible verses on forgiveness and ruminate on them daily.

Practicing Forgiveness:

a. Recall a past situation where you forgave your partner. How did it affect your relationship and personal wellbeing?

b. Are there any ongoing forgiveness challenges in your relationship that you need to address? If yes, discuss strategies to overcome them.

c. Commit to practicing forgiveness regularly and monitor the positive impact it has on your relationship.

Self-Reflection:

a. Reflect on your own ability to forgive. Are there any personal barriers or past experiences that make forgiveness difficult for you?

b. How can you work on overcoming these barriers and cultivating a mindset of forgiveness?

c. What self-care practices can you engage in to maintain emotional wellbeing and support the forgiveness process?

Remember, building healthy habits of forgiveness takes time and effort. Be patient with yourself and your partner as you navigate through these challenges and work on building forgiveness in your relationship.

MAIN IDEAS

Let's return to Hailey and Justin's story. The two of them recognized the need for positive changes in their relationship, as they noticed that their lack of trust and mutual respect was slowly eroding the foundation they had once built. To rebuild their connection, they consciously prioritized spending quality time together. They dedicated specific moments to reconnecting and understanding each other on a deeper level, aiming to reignite the fading spark in their relationship. Engaging in activities that promoted open communication and shared experiences became their way of rebuilding their emotional bond and rediscovering their passion.

In addition, Hailey and Justin embraced the transformative power of forgiveness. They actively chose to let go of past hurts and made an effort to understand each other's perspectives. By practicing forgiveness, they broke free from their destructive cycle of behavior and created a safe space for understanding and personal growth within their relationship. With each positive step they took, their commitment to building healthier habits grew stronger, leading them toward a more profound and fulfilling connection.

Healthy relationship habits are essential for cultivating meaningful and strong relationships. Prioritizing quality time, expressing gratitude, and practicing forgiveness are all examples of these habits. You and your partner can strengthen your bond and build a deeper emotional connection by setting out devoted moments for each other, away from distractions. Activities that promote open communication and shared experiences increase closeness and lead to a joyful and balanced relationship. Furthermore, expressing gratitude for one another creates a pleasant and supportive environment, reaffirming your mutual love and respect. Finally, practicing forgiveness allows you to move on while overcoming problems, providing a place of understanding and personal progress. By actively incorporating these healthy habits into your relationship, you can foster a stronger and more harmonious partnership that stands the test of time.

WORKBOOK SIX

Section 1: Reflecting on Your Relationship
1.1 Relationship Assessment:

- Rate the overall satisfaction and fulfillment in your relationship on a scale of 1 to 10.

- Identify the key areas that you feel need improvement in your relationship.

- Reflect on the current habits and patterns that contribute to both the beauty and the challenges in your relationship.

1.2 Identifying Healthy Habits:

- List three healthy habits that you believe are important for building a strong relationship.

- Describe how each of these habits contributes to a positive and fulfilling partnership.

- Reflect on whether you and your partner currently practice these habits consistently.

Section 2: Communication and Emotional Connection
2.1 Quality Time:

- Reflect on how much dedicated quality time you and your partner currently spend together.

- Identify any barriers or distractions that prevent you from having meaningful time together.

- Set a goal for increasing the amount and quality of your shared time. List specific activities or routines you can implement to achieve this goal.

2.2 Effective Communication:

- Assess the current state of communication in your relationship.

- Identify any communication patterns or behaviors that hinder open and effective communication.

- List three strategies or techniques that can improve your communication with your partner.

Section 3: Gratitude and Appreciation
3.1 Expressing Gratitude:

- Reflect on how frequently you express gratitude towards your partner.

- Identify specific qualities, actions, or efforts of your partner that you appreciate.

- Set a goal for expressing gratitude more consistently. List ways you can actively show appreciation to your partner on a regular basis.

3.2 Gratitude Reflection:

- Take turns with your partner to share three things you are grateful for about each other.

- Discuss how expressing and receiving gratitude positively impacts your relationship.

- Explore ways to integrate gratitude into your daily routine as a couple.

Section 4: Forgiveness
4.1 Cultivating Forgiveness:

- Reflect on your personal ability to forgive and let go of past hurts.

- Discuss with your partner the importance of forgiveness in your relationship.

- Set goals for cultivating forgiveness, both towards your partner and within yourself. List specific actions or practices you can undertake to promote forgiveness.

Remember, building healthy habits in your relationship is an ongoing process. Revisit this workbook periodically to assess your progress, refine your goals, and continue nurturing a strong and fulfilling partnership. Don't forget to pray!

PART THREE

Coping with Anxiety for Long-Lasting Happiness in Your Relationship

In the first and second parts of this book, you gained an understanding of what anxiety and overthinking are (especially relationship anxiety); you were also introduced to strategies by which you can manage anxiety and overthinking and prevent it from damaging your relationship. In this third part, you'll be introduced to how you can cope with your anxiety and overthinking in order to achieve long-lasting happiness. This part includes:

- Decluttering your way to happiness
- Coping strategies that work

First, we'll look at the ability of decluttering to create a more peaceful and fulfilling environment, both externally and internally. Then, we will give you tried-and-true coping skills for dealing with anxiety and overthinking, helping you to create a happier and better relationship. Prepare to embark on the road to lasting happiness!

CHAPTER SEVEN

Decluttering Your Way to Happiness

"To everything there is a season, A time for every purpose under heaven."

—Ecclesiastes 3:1

Alayna had always been a meticulous person, obsessing over every detail in her life, especially in her romantic relationships. Her mind was cluttered with worries, doubts, and endless overthinking about her partner's actions and intentions. It took a toll on her happiness and strained the connection she had with her partner. One day, while tidying up her apartment, she stumbled upon a book about decluttering both physical spaces and the mind. Intrigued, she decided to give it a try.

In today's fast-paced and jam-packed world, our lives are often loaded with an overwhelming quantity of information, possessions, and duties. And while we struggle to make sense of our chaotic reality, we may discover that we have neglected both our thoughts and our physical spaces, causing them to become crowded with irrelevant thoughts, ideas, and trinkets. The effects of this clutter, though, may go well beyond our physical surroundings; it can seep into our relationships, causing anxiety and overthinking that puts unnecessary strain on the connection.

Clutter in our lives may take many forms, ranging from physical clutter in our houses to mental clutter that hampers our thoughts and emotions.

This is when the habit of decluttering comes in handy. Decluttering is more than just cleaning up our physical environment; it is a transforming process that involves letting go of the unwanted baggage we carry in our minds. By actively decluttering our minds and spaces, we may find it easier to create space for joy, calm, and true connections in our relationships and to manage the anxiety and overthinking that weigh us down.

Understanding Mental Clutter

We have become used to regarding the stressed-out, overwhelmed, and negative feelings we sometimes get as part of life. Despite its effect on our lives and mental state, we just shrug and go on with our day thinking it's quite normal. But it isn't—it is a damaging state of being that lessens productivity and affects the way we live and interact with others. This is known as mental clutter.

Just as physical clutter in our home can make us feel overwhelmed "mental clutter is anything that makes our minds feel like they're on overdrive" (Daisy, 2020). So, what is mental clutter? It's "the excess thoughts and ideas that crowd your mind and prevent you from thinking clearly or focusing on your tasks at hand" (Jenna, 2023). It can show up as a never-ending stream of negative self-talk, racing thoughts, and/or a heightened sensation of uncertainty and fear. Mental clutter can have a negative impact on our emotional wellbeing, capacity to communicate effectively, and overall relationship satisfaction.

Mental clutter sometimes appears as anxiety and overthinking in the context of relationships. It can cause uncertainty, insecurity, and an insatiable need for acceptance. This mental state can damage relationships by producing misunderstandings, disagreements, and a lack of trust.

Mental clutter can occur in a variety of ways, and the way it shows up varies from person to person. Here are some common manifestations of mental clutter:

1. Racing thoughts: Your mind may be continually bombarded with a barrage of thoughts, making it difficult to focus or maintain mental stillness. These ideas could be repetitive, invasive, or unfavorable.

2. Overthinking: Overanalyzing and ruminating on past or current events, or what might happen in the future, is a common source of mental clutter. This can result in a loop of rumination and an inability to make solid decisions.

3. Anxiety and worry: Mental clutter may contribute to increased worry and anxiety. You may become anxious about numerous areas of your relationship, such as the partnership's stability, your partner's feelings, or possible conflicts.

4. Negative self-talk: Negative internal talk is a part of having mental clutter. You may criticize yourself, doubt your own worth, or constantly question your actions and intentions in the relationship. ·

5. Catastrophic thinking: Mental clutter can lead to a tendency to imagine worst-case scenarios or to overanalyze circumstances. This may worsen anxiety and create a sense of unease and uncertainty in the relationship.

Decluttering Is Self-Care

"Hey, I can't find my anxiety. You didn't throw it out, did you?"

When we think of self-care, activities such as relaxing by a pool, going to the spa, and engaging in hobbies often come to mind. While these are all great forms of taking care of yourself, you need to remember to take care of your mental wellbeing, too (Poplin, 2022). Decluttering may not be an exciting process—after all, nobody wants to tackle that overflowing sock drawer, and nobody wants to have to face what's going on in their head—but still, it is an essential part of self-care. Self-care activities should nurture both your physical and your emotional health (Colino, 2022).

Physical decluttering, therefore, is a deliberate act of self-care that may have a significant influence on your mental and emotional health. Here are a few ways that decluttering might benefit you:

1. Improved mental clarity: Crowded surroundings can lead to a cluttered mind. It might be difficult to concentrate and think clearly when your physical environment is unorganized and chaotic. You can create a more beneficial atmosphere for mental clarity and productivity by cleaning and arranging your space. When that overflowing sock drawer is eventually sorted out, your mind won't keep on going back to it when you're supposed to be working (especially if you're working from home where it can be easily seen).

2. Reduced tension: Clutter can be a substantial cause of tension. It overwhelms our senses, intensifies visual distractions, and causes mental and emotional heaviness. Decluttering helps you to recover control and order in your daily activities, lowering stress and encouraging a better sense of quiet and serenity.

3. Increased productivity and efficiency: Physical and mental clutter alike may make it difficult to be productive and effective. We can reduce distractions, better utilize our resources, and create a more efficient and structured workflow by decluttering. This frees up mental energy and makes room for more intense and productive tasks.

Benefits of Decluttering for Your Mental Health

Why do we need to declutter? "If the physical space around us feels scattered, it's likely our mental space will feel the same" (Beckwith & Parkhurst, 2022). Decluttering can have significant benefits for your mental health, particularly in relation to anxiety and overthinking. Here are some key benefits of decluttering:

1. Increased self-esteem and confidence: Decluttering might help you feel better about yourself. You will feel more accomplished and empowered as you take charge of your environment and regulate your thoughts more efficiently. This can lead to higher self-esteem and confidence in other aspects of your life, such as your relationships.

2. Emotional wellbeing: Clutter can elicit negative feelings and memories connected with prior experiences or unsolved problems. Decluttering allows you to let go of physical belongings as well as mental baggage, making room for pleasant emotions and a stronger sense of emotional wellbeing. It allows you to concentrate on the current moment and build a more cheerful and happy attitude.

3. Improved sleep quality: Sleep can be disrupted by an overactive mind packed with clutter and racing thoughts. Decluttering contributes to a more tranquil

and serene bedroom atmosphere, which promotes relaxation and good sleep. You can wake up feeling more refreshed and invigorated by eliminating physical and mental clutter before bed.

4. Improved relationship: Mental clutter can cause tension and strain in relationships. Decluttering creates a more harmonic and serene environment, which promotes greater communication and understanding. Furthermore, reducing overthinking and worry allows you to be more present and attentive to your partner's demands, boosting the quality of your interactions.

Decluttering Your Mind: A How-To Guide

Your mind has an enormous influence over your daily experiences. However, it can easily get overwhelmed by the sheer volume of information and thoughts it processes at times. In such cases, your cognitive capacity may deteriorate, making it harder to think clearly, make informed decisions, and retain productivity. Furthermore, negativity can impair your mental and emotional wellbeing. To be honest, finding effective strategies to clean and restore mental clarity can be a difficult task—but not to worry, here are some simple ways to start decluttering your mind:

1. Set priorities: Making a list of priorities allows you to "take all those thoughts and decisions and put them

into action" (Solvere Living, 2023). Prioritization is a necessary discipline for decluttering the mind, enabling you to effectively filter out distractions and focus on tasks that align with your goals because you're keeping in mind what genuinely matters and merits your attention. It allows you to intelligently manage your limited mental resources, make informed decisions, boost your productivity, and retain clear thinking. Setting priorities is a useful tool for navigating life's difficulties and ensuring that your efforts are focused on what is truly important.

2. Exercise regularly: Regular exercise is an effective approach to cleansing your mind. Physical activity relieves stress and tension by increasing endorphin levels and generating a happy mental state. This improves mental clarity and provides an outlet for any pent-up emotions. It also improves overall mental wellbeing, focus, and concentration, and creates calmer and more balanced thinking. The physical and mental relaxation caused by exercise will allow you to tackle challenging tasks and situations with renewed vigor and clarity.

3. Transfer your thoughts to paper: Writing down the jumble of thoughts in your mind can be a very helpful way to mentally declutter (Eisler, 2019). Writing down your problems, for example, allows you to externalize

them and acquire clarity. It assists in processing emotions, reflecting on experiences, and organizing your thoughts. Writing your thoughts in a diary provides a secure and private space to offload your mental burdens, reducing overwhelm and encouraging mental order. Journaling on a regular basis allows you to gain insights, detect trends in your behavior, and develop a better self-understanding.

4. Learn to let go: "Accept yourself, love yourself, and keep moving forward" (Nazish, 2017). Accepting yourself, including your shortcomings and flaws, frees you from the burden of self-judgment and comparison. Adopting self-love allows you to cultivate inner serenity. Furthermore, by letting go of the past and focusing on the future, you divert your attention away from past mistakes or unfavorable experiences and towards personal development and self-improvement. This approach motivates you to establish objectives, learn from setbacks, and strive for constant improvement.

5. Seek support: Seeking help is another effective approach to clearing your mind. You can create a safe space for free dialogue and emotional expression by reaching out to trustworthy individuals such as friends, family members, or a therapist. Sharing your feelings

and thoughts with others can help you gain perspective, validate your experiences, and let go of any pent-up stress or anxiety. When you seek help, you allow understanding and empathy into your life, which relieves the stress of having to handle everything on your own. Engaging in meaningful conversations with people and receiving direction or advice from them can give clarity and fresh insights. It also increases your sense of connection and creates a support network on which you may rely in difficult times.

Decluttering Your Space

Are you envious of the spotless, clutter-free houses featured on home décor blogs and websites? Minimalist spaces and the promise of decluttering tactics can be appealing. I'm sure it's no surprise to you by now that decluttering can have a major influence not only on your physical space but also on your general wellbeing—but is simplicity genuinely livable? The answer is yes, if you make the required effort.

Decluttering extends beyond simply cleaning up your physical surroundings. It entails deliberately organizing and removing unneeded stuff in order to create a more practical and harmonious living environment. It frees up physical space, making it easier to access the items you need. This increases efficiency while decreasing the time and stress associated with looking for misplaced things. Furthermore, a clutter-free environment can boost productivity and focus, allowing you to complete activities with greater ease and concentration.

Decluttering also offers emotional benefits. It can be freeing to let go of belongings that no longer serve a purpose or have sentimental value. It allows you to make room for new experiences and memories, as well as promotes a sense of rejuvenation and growth. To declutter your space:

- Consider dividing objects into categories such as "keep," "donate," or "toss" to efficiently declutter your home.

- Consider the benefits of living with less and what genuinely brings worth to your life.

- Simplify your storage methods, create routines for keeping things organized, and fight the need to amass unnecessary objects in the future.

Taking Digital Detoxes

What is a digital detox?

One definition of a digital detox is "to take a break from using electronic devices or certain media for a period of time, from a few days to several months" (Cleveland Clinic, 2021). Here are some things to avoid while on a digital detox:

- Social media

- Email and messaging apps for anything other than work

- Online recreation
- News consumption
- TV

The most common type of digital detox is a vacation from looking at or engaging in social media. Negative social media encounters can cause anxiety and despair, as well as lower self-esteem. This includes the following:

- Becoming upset or disturbed by the things you see
- Cyberbullying (verbal bullying on the internet)
- Comparisons on a social level

The Advantages of Digital Detoxes:

Digital detoxification is an important strategy in today's technology-driven environment. It involves purposefully separating yourself from the digital world in order to establish a healthier and more balanced relationship with technology, and this has multiple advantages for your mental and emotional health.

Digital detoxing has been shown to improve real-life connections and relationships. Constant digital distractions might make it difficult to engage in meaningful connections with others. You will have more time and attention to dedicate to face-to-face talks, quality time with loved ones, and indulging in things that bring you joy and fulfillment if you step away from screens.

Furthermore, digital detoxes encourage better sleep. The blue light emitted by screens has been shown to disturb our natural sleep cycles and sleep quality. By disconnecting from digital gadgets before bedtime, you create a relaxing environment and increase your chances of getting a good night's sleep.

Signs that you should put down your gadget:

Do you think you need a digital detox? If you encounter any of the following when using electronic media, then it may be time to disconnect:

- Irritability, frustration, or anger
- Feeling uneasy
- Sleep deprivation or interruption
- Comparison to others
- An obligation to consume, reply, react, or check in
- Fear of missing out

How to do a digital detox (some of the information below has been drawn from the Cleveland Clinic, 2021):

1. Decide on what you want to change: It is critical to first identify the exact behavior or habits you intend to change. This might include excessive social media use,

frequently checking emails or notifications, spending too much time playing video games, or any other digital activity that you believe is affecting your wellbeing or productivity.

2. Reduce your fear of missing out: Don't worry, you're not alone in this feeling (Tuca, 2023). Training ourselves to overcome the fear of missing out (FOMO) and the sense of urgency that frequently drives our ongoing digital involvement is a key component of undergoing a digital detox. While detoxing, you may experience anxiety about missing out on something important or exciting that is happening online, whether it's a social event, a news update, or even the everyday routines of your friends and acquaintances. To solve this, it's critical to remember that disconnecting from your devices will not cause the world to stop spinning. Remind yourself that disconnecting from digital platforms does not imply missing out on life; rather, it helps you to completely engage with the current moment and concentrate on your own wellbeing and personal growth.

3. Reflect on yourself: Take regular breaks during your digital detox to reflect on your progress and how the detox is affecting your life. Take note of any changes in your mood, energy level, productivity, and general wellbeing. Self-reflection will enable you to assess the

benefits of limiting digital consumption and to reaffirm your commitment to a healthier relationship with technology.

4. Find alternatives: Finding alternative activities to replace the time you would normally spend on digital devices is a critical component of a good digital detox. Look for hobbies or interests that you have ignored or would like to pursue further, such as reading, exercising, spending time in nature, pursuing creative outlets such as painting or playing a musical instrument, or simply spending quality time with loved ones. Experiment with different activities to identify those that provide joy, relaxation, or a sense of accomplishment. Engaging in these new activities will not only help divert you from digital temptations, but will also provide a rewarding and engaging experience during your detox.

Habits for Happiness in Your Relationship

There are several general habits you can adopt that may help boost your happiness and overall wellbeing (and, therefore, your relationship satisfaction as well). Here are several examples:

1. Smile: Smiling is a natural outward expression of happiness (Pietrangelo, 2023). It's also a simple and

effective method of improving your mood and bringing more happiness into your life. When you're genuinely happy, you probably smile. What's remarkable is that by smiling consciously, you can actually activate emotions of happiness and improve your mood. Have you ever wondered why, when you're with friends, you laugh at things you usually wouldn't find funny? That's because smiling and laughing are contagious. When you smile at others, you almost always get a smile back, resulting in a positive social encounter and creating a sense of connection and belonging. A simple smile can strengthen your interpersonal relationships, give you an approachable demeanor, and even boost your professional relationships.

2. Practice mindfulness: Being fully present and aware of the current moment without judgment is what mindfulness is all about. You can improve your sense of peace and happiness by practicing this habit.

3. Perform acts of kindness: Being good to others might boost your own happiness. Small acts of kindness, such as assisting someone in need or expressing thanks, not only benefit others but also generate a sense of purpose and satisfaction within yourself.

4. Have optimism: Developing an optimistic mindset means focusing on the positive, keeping hope alive, and having a positive outlook on life. You can build better

happiness and resilience by reframing obstacles as opportunities and adopting a growth mindset.

Practicing Happiness Worksheet

1. Gratitude Reflection:

- List three things you appreciate about your relationship.

- List another three things you appreciate specifically about your partner.

- Reflect on how expressing gratitude can help you let go of anxiety and overthinking.

2. Positive Self-Talk:

- Write down three positive affirmations about yourself and your relationship.

- How can incorporating positive self-talk contribute to reducing anxiety and promoting happiness?

3. Letting Go Exercise:

- Identify one anxiety-inducing thought or overthinking pattern related to your relationship.

- Challenge and reframe that thought with a more realistic and positive perspective.

- Talk to your partner about this thought and discuss it sincerely with them.

- Reflect on how letting go of negative thoughts can enhance your overall happiness and wellbeing.

4. Acts of Kindness:

- Brainstorm three acts of kindness you can perform for your partner.

- Take action and complete one act of kindness this week.

- Reflect on how spreading kindness enhances your relationship and contributes to your own happiness.

5. Joyful Moments Journal:

- Set aside a few minutes each day to write down moments of joy or happiness in your relationship.

- Describe the situation, your feelings, and why it brought you happiness.

- Review your journal regularly to remind yourself of the positive aspects of your relationship.

6. Self-Care Plan:

- Create a self-care plan that is specifically tailored to reducing anxiety and promoting happiness in your relationship.

- List activities or practices that bring you joy, relaxation, and rejuvenation.

- Schedule regular self-care practices and commit to implementing them.

- Try carrying out these exercises with your partner and reflect on how this affects you both.

Remember, the purpose of this worksheet is to assist you in actively practicing happiness and letting go of worry and overthinking in your relationship. Take the time to complete each activity carefully and reflect on how it affects your wellbeing.

MAIN IDEAS

Let's return to Alayna. Inspired by a great book she had read, Alayna embarked on a journey of self-reflection and letting go. She started by acknowledging her anxious thoughts and their impact on her romantic relationship. Gradually, she learned to recognize when her mind was spiraling into overthinking mode. With patience and practice, she began detaching herself from unnecessary worries, releasing the grip of anxiety that had held her captive for so long. As she let go of cluttered thoughts, her connection with her partner blossomed. She embraced vulnerability, communicated more openly, and allowed herself to trust and be fully present in the relationship. With each step, Alayna discovered that decluttering her mind was the key to unlocking happiness and fostering a deeper, more fulfilling bond with her loved ones.

To declutter your way to happiness, you must simplify and organize all elements of your life in order to create a more harmonious and serene environment. Cleaning your physical space lowers tension and promotes a sense of serenity. Furthermore, giving up material goods that no longer serve a function can provide a sense of release and make room for new experiences.

In addition to physical clutter, decluttering your mental and emotional space is essential. Let go of negative thinking, poisonous relationships, and bad behaviors. By decluttering, you make room for more clarity, focus, and, eventually, happiness.

WORKBOOK SEVEN

Part 1: Mind Decluttering

1. Identify Mental Clutter:

- Take a moment to reflect on any recurring negative thoughts, worries, or mental distractions that contribute to clutter in your mind.

- Write down three specific examples of mental clutter that you would like to address.

2. Challenge Negative Thoughts:

- Choose one negative thought related to your relationship from your list.

- Write down evidence that supports and contradicts this thought.

- Create a more balanced and realistic perspective by considering the evidence against the negative thought.

3. Journaling:

- Start a journal to unload your thoughts and emotions.

- Write freely, without judgment or expectation.

- Use the journal as a tool to declutter your mind and gain clarity.

4. Practice Self-Compassion:

- Write down three affirmations or positive statements about yourself and your relationship.

- Repeat these affirmations daily as a reminder to be kind to yourself and let go of self-criticism.

Part 2: Space Decluttering

1. Assess Your Environment:

- Look around your living space and identify areas that feel cluttered and overwhelming.

- Write down three specific areas or items that you want to declutter.

2. Decluttering Plan:

- Develop a plan of action to tackle each area or item.

- Break it down into smaller tasks and set a timeline for completion.

- Consider enlisting the help of your partner for support.

3. Sorting and Organizing:

- Start decluttering one area at a time.

- Sort items into categories: keep, donate/sell, or discard.

- Find proper storage solutions for the items you decide to keep.

4. Simplify Your Space:

- Embrace minimalism by removing unnecessary items and keeping only what brings you joy or serves a purpose.

- Create a peaceful and organized space that promotes relaxation and clarity.

5. Maintenance:

- Develop habits to maintain a clutter-free environment.

- Set a regular schedule for decluttering and tidying up your space.

Remember, decluttering your mind and space is an ongoing process. Be patient with yourself and celebrate small victories along the way. As you declutter, you create space for more peace, clarity, and positive energy in your life.

CHAPTER EIGHT

Coping Strategies That Work

"Look at the birds of the air, for they neither sow nor reap nor gather into barns; yet your heavenly Father feeds them. Are you not of more value than they?"

—Matthew 6:26

"Focus on what you can control and let go of what is beyond your control. Release the need to fix everything and trust in the process of life and relationships."

—Eckhart Tolle

Ariana had always been a worrier, often finding it difficult to let go of her worries and fully immerse herself in her relationships. This negatively affected not only her mental health, but also her relationships. One day, Ariana attended a personal development workshop and was immediately impressed by one of the speakers, Jane. Drawn to Jane's calm demeanor and the way she seemed to have insight into Ariana's inner thoughts, Ariana mustered the courage to approach her after the session. She poured her heart out, sharing her struggles with anxiety and the impact it had on her relationships.

Jane listened attentively, empathizing with Ariana's journey. Drawing from her own experience, she shared the coping strategies that had transformed his life and relationships. Jane emphasized the power of self-compassion, urging Ariana to be kind to herself and challenge her self-critical thoughts. She encouraged her to engage in activities that brought her joy, fostering a sense of balance and fulfillment.

Anxiety may easily take hold of our lives in today's demanding society, hurting not just our personal wellbeing but also our relationships with others. Constant anxiety, self-doubt, and overthinking may block true connections, leaving us craving efficient coping skills that might bring us closer to inner peace and deepen our relationships. This is when the effectiveness of coping mechanisms comes into play.

Coping strategies are techniques and methods that assist us in navigating the difficulties of anxiety and cultivating healthy relationships. They give us the ability to release ourselves from anxiety's grip, allowing us to be completely present in our relationships and create stronger connections. These strategies do not aim to avoid or suppress our emotions, but rather to build up resilience and self-awareness in order to navigate them with grace and authenticity.

Safety Behaviors Are Unhealthy

It is critical to realize the impact of safety habits when it comes to managing anxiety and developing healthy relationships. We all develop these behaviors to cope with our anxieties and uncertainties, seeking control and relief. Basically, "safety behaviors are used in an attempt to prevent fears from coming true and to feel more comfortable in fearful situations" (Qhek, 2022). However, it is critical to recognize that relying on safety habits can be detrimental in the long term, both for ourselves and for our relationships (Peterson, 2018).

Safety habits, you see, may briefly ease our anxiety and provide us with a temporary feeling of control, but they prevent us from confronting and overcoming our worries over time. They reinforce our belief that the things we are afraid of are genuinely dangerous, keeping us in an anxiety loop. Furthermore, safety behaviors can strain our relationships by instilling in us an unhealthy dependence on reassurance-seeking or by limiting our ability to fully participate in shared events.

Recognizing and addressing these safety habits is critical for breaking free from the hold of anxiety and fostering healthy relationships. It requires bravery to question the assumptions that underpin them and progressively diminish our reliance on them. Seeking professional treatment, such as therapy or counseling, may be extremely beneficial in creating alternative coping methods that promote emotional wellbeing and encourage confronting our concerns.

By letting go of safety habits, we create a deeper feeling of self-trust and resilience, making room for personal development and the chance to meet life's obstacles with bravery. We develop open communication, vulnerability, and trust in our relationships by letting go of incessant reassurance-seeking and adopting a healthy perspective. Here are the most common types of safety behaviors to look out for.

1. Avoidance: Avoidance refers to purposefully avoiding circumstances, locations, or people that cause uneasiness. To alleviate discomfort, for example, someone suffering from social anxiety may shun social outings or opportunities for public speaking. While avoidance may bring short respite, it promotes the notion that the dreaded scenario is genuinely harmful, making long-term anxiety management challenging.

2. Dependency on reassurance: Individuals may seek excessive reassurance from others in order to reduce their uneasiness. They may continuously want affirmation, comfort, or confirmation that everything is fine. While seeking support is a natural aspect of every relationship, relying on reassurance excessively can strain your relationship and foster dependency by reinforcing the need for external validation to handle your anxiety.

3. Checking habits: Checking habits entail continuously examining and rechecking items to ensure safety or prevent injury—for example, repeatedly inspecting locks, appliances, or personal possessions to ensure their security.

4. Rituals and compulsions: Another sort of safety behavior is engaging in rituals or obsessive actions. These rituals may consist of precise action sequences or repetitive behaviors targeted at alleviating anxiety. Excessive handwashing, organizing items in a precise order, or repeating certain phrases are examples.

Healthy vs. Unhealthy Coping Skills

"Well this is boring. I'll go find someone else to play with!"

Coping skills are methods by which we can better deal with stress, anxiety, and uncomfortable emotions. Healthy coping skills play an essential role in your relationship to help you overcome challenges, develop resilience, and maintain emotional wellbeing. However, it is crucial to distinguish between healthy and unhealthy coping skills, as the latter can worsen anxiety and overthinking rather than alleviate it. Let's take a closer look:

1. Healthy coping skills: Healthy coping skills promote emotional wellbeing and contribute to the general health of your relationship. They are adaptable, constructive, and efficient in dealing with stress and worry. Here are a few examples:

   ▪ Self-care: Exercise, getting adequate sleep, eating healthy meals, consciously taking proper care of yourself, and practicing relaxation methods are all examples of self-care activities that can help reduce anxiety and positively affect the state of your health and relationship. Taking care of your physical and mental health is essential for having a positive attitude in your relationship.

   ▪ Communication: Healthy relationships require open and honest communication. Communication can make or break a relationship. Expressing your opinions, thoughts, and feelings in a transparent and polite manner promotes efficient problem-solving and mutual understanding. Active listening and assertiveness are two communication skills that can help minimize misunderstandings and lessen anxiety in relationships.

- Setting boundaries: Maintaining a balanced and respectful dynamic in your relationship requires the establishment of appropriate boundaries— emphasis on appropriate! Be aware that it is possible to use boundaries the wrong way and turn them into a safety strategy, one that enables you to push your loved ones away. Appropriate boundary-setting entails identifying your personal boundaries and conveying them to your partner. This protects your wellbeing and ensures that both parties feel at ease, protected, and appreciated.

2. Unhealthy coping techniques: On the other side, unhealthy coping techniques may offer momentary solace but ultimately worsen anxiety and overanalyzing in relationships. They are regressive and may be detrimental to emotional health. Here are a few examples:

- Precautions: It is possible to experience a momentary reprieve from tension or conflict by avoiding or repressing emotions and trying circumstances. But ignoring issues rather than dealing with them head-on might eventually result in unsolved problems, animosity, and elevated anxiety.

- Substance abuse: Using alcohol or other drugs to deal with stress or worry is a bad coping strategy. Abuse of substances can exacerbate mental health conditions, lead to new issues, and damage relationships.

- Excessive control: Excessive control can result from anxiety and insecurity, as can the need to manage every element of a relationship or a partner's ongoing need for affirmation. This excessive need for control undermines emotional intimacy and trust while also causing overthinking and anxiety.

It's important to recognize that everyone may exhibit both healthy and unhealthy coping skills at different times. However, the goal is to cultivate self-awareness and actively work towards replacing unhealthy coping mechanisms with healthier alternatives.

Self-Soothing Exercises

Self-soothing "is an emotional regulation strategy used to regain equilibrium after an upsetting event" (Nash, 2022). It should be noted that the overuse or improper use of self-soothing strategies can lead to emotional avoidance, disruption of intimate relationships, or unhealthy safety behaviors, as discussed earlier (Schwartz, 2022; Nash, 2022). These strategies "are meant to be short-term, temporary tools to allow a person to overcome difficult situations and negative emotions" (Schwartz, 2022).

Self-soothing has numerous benefits. First, it "activates the parasympathetic nervous [system], helping to decrease symptoms of anxiety, stress, and panic," thereby reducing impulsivity and helping you to pay attention to what's happening in the moment (Schwartz, 2022).

You can foster a better relationship with both yourself and your partner and improve your general wellbeing by implementing self-soothing exercises into your daily routine. Let's dive deeper into a few self-calming exercises:

1. Breathing techniques: Practice deep breathing by paying attention to your breath for a while. Exercises that include deep breathing are really easy to do but effective at promoting calm. Get into a comfortable posture and take a slow, deep breath through your nose, letting your belly expand. Release any tension or stress by exhaling slowly through your mouth. Do this for several minutes while feeling the peaceful rhythm of your breath. You may quickly and effectively reduce anxiety by practicing deep breathing anywhere, at any time.

2. Progressive muscle relaxation: When you experience stress in your body, progressive muscle relaxation can help you release it. Begin by tensing a specific muscle area, such as your shoulders, for a few seconds, and then deliberately release the tension while focusing on the sense of relaxation and relief it brings. Do the same for different muscle groups. This helps you to relax as you become more aware of your body.

3. Guided imagination: Allow your mind to transport you to a serene place—somewhere that brings you a sense of calm and tranquility. It could be a peaceful and warm beach with the ocean breeze all around you, a breathtaking garden, or a quaint cottage in the mountains. It can be a place you've been to, a place that you link with relaxation, maybe that place you visited on a vacation and had a great time. Think about the feelings you experienced while you were there, the person or people you were with, and the sense of relaxation and camaraderie that was present. Engage all your senses in this visualization, noticing the sights, sounds, smells, and textures around you. Allow yourself to be fully present in this soothing mental image, letting go of any anxieties that may be weighing on your mind.

Breathing Exercises

Breathing exercises are powerful tools that can help us manage anxiety and overthinking in various aspects of life, including relationships. When we feel overwhelmed or anxious, our breathing often becomes shallow and rapid, contributing to a cycle of stress and negative thinking. Engaging in specific breathing exercises can help break this cycle by activating the body's relaxation response and promoting a sense of calm and emotional balance.

Anxiety causes us "to take rapid, shallow breaths that come directly from the chest" (Ankrom, 2023). This "causes an upset in the body's oxygen and carbon dioxide levels, resulting in increased heart rate, dizziness, muscle tension, and other physical sensations," which may even lead to panic attacks (Ankrom, 2023).

Diaphragmatic or deep breathing, on the other hand, allows you to calm yourself when you're in a scary or anxiety-inducing situation (Ankrom, 2023). Breathe deeply into your abdomen, not shallowly into your chest. Find a quiet and comfortable area to sit or lie down to do this breathing exercise. Place one hand on your stomach and the other on your chest. Allow your stomach to rise as you take a deep breath. Hold for a few seconds, then exhale through your lips, allowing your stomach to return to its regular position. Repeat many times, focusing on how your breath enters and exits your body.

Deep belly breathing like this can assist in calming your nervous system and activating your body's relaxation response. By doing this on purpose, we communicate to our brain that we are safe and in charge. Because it reduces the physiological response associated with stress, it can help ease feelings of anxiety.

Another beneficial breathing technique is "4-7-8" breathing. This method was developed by Dr. Andrew Weil to help manage breathing and promote a sensation of serenity. To practice this, close your eyes and sit comfortably. Count to four while inhaling deeply through your nose. For seven counts, hold your breath. Then, for eight counts, slowly exhale through your lips.

Another effective breathing technique is called "equal breathing." This exercise involves inhaling and exhaling for an equal count, promoting a sense of equilibrium and inner calm. To practice this technique, find a comfortable position and begin by taking a slow, deep breath in through your nose, counting to four. Then, exhale slowly through your nose for the same count of four. Continue this rhythmic breathing pattern for several minutes, focusing on the gentle rise and fall of your breath.

Equal breathing aids in the regulation of the autonomic nerve system, which regulates our body's stress reaction. We engage the parasympathetic nerve system by actively coordinating our breathing and exhalation, which counteracts the "fight or flight" reaction and produces calm. This technique may be especially helpful in relationships during difficult or uncomfortable situations because it helps us to answer from a position of calm and clarity rather than reacting impulsively out of fear.

Practicing Journaling

If you have been paying attention, you will have noticed that I've mentioned journaling several times in this book. There's a reason why. There is something especially soothing and relaxing about putting your thoughts and emotions to paper. It helps us look at and assess our thoughts differently than when they're only in our heads. It's also "the cheapest form of therapy because it is so therapeutic to perform a brain-dump" (Vidakovic, 2023). It offers the opportunity to problem-solve as you sort through various worries and to let go of what you can't control (Feyoh, 2023).

However, these benefits don't occur automatically or immediately. There comes first a sense of temporary relief, the kind that comes with letting go of something huge or burdening. However, over time, as you read what you've written over again, you'll begin to assess those words differently and eventually have different thoughts and come up with alternative viewpoints.

Journal Prompts

A journal "is a record of significant experiences and [is] used to explore ideas that take shape" (Vidakovic, 2023). Journaling can help you avoid "drowning in [your] own fearful thoughts" (Feyoh, 2023). Below are some useful journaling prompts you can use in managing your anxiety and overthinking, especially when it comes to your relationship (some prompts are taken from Feyoh, 2023; Vidakovic, 2023):

1. What three things scare you the most and why? When you face the things that scare you, you take from them the ability to cause anxiety and/or overthinking in you. You give them less power over your life and relationship.

2. List your current worries in life.

3. Reflect on a recent situation where anxiety or overthinking affected your relationship. What were the triggers that intensified these feelings? How did they manifest in your thoughts, emotions, and behaviors?

4. Describe a specific fear or worry you often experience in your relationship. What evidence do you have to support this fear? Are there any alternative perspectives or explanations that you can consider?

5. Explore the patterns of overthinking that tend to emerge in your relationship. What repetitive thoughts

or scenarios occupy your mind? How do they impact your overall wellbeing and the dynamics of your relationship?

6. Identify three negative beliefs or self-limiting thoughts that contribute to anxiety or overthinking in your relationship. Where do these beliefs originate from, and how do they affect your perception of yourself and your partner?

7. Consider the role of self-compassion in letting go of anxiety and overthinking. How can you cultivate a more compassionate and understanding attitude towards yourself in moments of relationship-related stress or uncertainty?

8. Write a letter to yourself, offering words of encouragement and support as you navigate your relationship challenges. What advice would you give to yourself to promote self-growth, resilience, and inner peace?

9. Explore the concept of acceptance in relationships. What aspects of your relationship do you struggle to accept? How might embracing acceptance contribute to reducing anxiety and overthinking?

10. Reflect on the impact of setting healthy boundaries in your relationship. Are there any specific boundaries you need to establish or reinforce? How can these

boundaries create a sense of safety and reduce anxiety
and overthinking?

Remember, journaling is personal and requires deep thinking.
Use these journal prompts as a way of managing your anxiety.
Ensure that you are honest with yourself, making your journal
a safe space—one that isn't used as a crutch.

MAIN IDEAS

Remember Ariana from the start of this chapter? As she
embarked on her path of letting go of anxiety and nurturing her
relationships, she embraced the coping strategies that Jane had
shared. She began practicing mindfulness, allowing herself to
fully experience each moment without judgment. Ariana also
incorporated self-care rituals into her daily routine, such as
engaging in creative pursuits and spending time in nature. Over
time, she noticed a profound shift within herself. The grip of
anxiety loosened, allowing her to be more present and attuned
to her loved ones.

She learned to communicate her feelings and needs with
authenticity, cultivating deeper connections built on trust and
understanding. Ariana's relationships flourished, enriched by
her newfound sense of inner peace and resilience. Through her
journey, she realized that coping strategies that work are not a
one-size-fits-all solution but a personalized exploration of self-
discovery and growth. By embracing these strategies and letting

go of anxiety, Ariana found herself on a transformative path towards vibrant relationships and a life filled with joy and fulfillment.

Developing effective coping strategies to let go of anxiety and overthinking in your relationship is a crucial step towards improving your mental health and building a healthier connection with your partner. It is also important that you're able to recognize and let go of the unhealthy safety behaviors that aggravate your anxiety. By consciously choosing self-soothing exercises such as deep breathing and journaling, you can find moments of peace and self-reflection amidst relationship challenges. Developing a personalized coping plan, assessing your progress, and adjusting your strategies along the way will enable you to fine-tune your approach and continue growing.

WORKBOOK EIGHT

Instructions: This is to help you create coping strategies that will allow you to build a relationship free from anxiety and overthinking. Answer each question truthfully, because this workbook is for your benefit.

Part 1: Understanding Your Triggers

    a. What are some common situations or events that trigger anxiety or overthinking in your relationship?

    b. How do these triggers affect your thoughts, emotions, and behaviors?

Part 2: Healthy Coping Strategies

    a. Self-Care and Stress Management:

- List three self-care activities that help you relax and recharge.

- How often do you currently engage in these activities? Are there any additional self-care practices you would like to incorporate?

    b. Effective Communication Techniques:

- Reflect on a recent situation where communication caused anxiety or overthinking. How could you have approached the situation differently to promote better communication and reduce anxiety?

- Identify two communication techniques you can practice to enhance your ability to express your thoughts and emotions effectively in your relationship.

c. Establishing Boundaries:

- In what areas of your relationship do you struggle with setting boundaries?

- Identify one boundary you would like to establish or reinforce. How will this boundary contribute to reducing anxiety and overthinking in your relationship?

d. Seeking Support:

- Who are the individuals in your life whom you trust and feel comfortable seeking support from when facing relationship-related anxieties or overthinking?

- Reflect on the importance of seeking professional support when needed. Are there any barriers or concerns preventing you from seeking professional help if necessary?

Part 3: Developing a Personalized Coping Plan

a. Unhealthy Safety Behaviors:

- Reflect on any unhealthy safety behaviors or coping mechanisms that you tend to rely on when experiencing anxiety or overthinking in your relationship.

- Identify three unhealthy safety behaviors you would like to let go of.

- Why do you believe these behaviors are detrimental to your wellbeing and relationship?

b. Deep Breathing Techniques:

- Practice a deep breathing exercise for a few minutes. Focus on inhaling deeply through your nose and exhaling slowly through your mouth.

- How do you feel after engaging in this exercise?

c. Self-Soothing Exercises:

- Choose one self-soothing exercise from this chapter or elsewhere that resonates with you. Describe the exercise and how it promotes relaxation and peace of mind.

d. Journaling:

- Reflect on the benefits of journaling as a self-soothing and self-reflective practice. Have you tried journaling before? If yes, how has it helped you? If not, are you open to giving it a try?

- Commit to incorporating journaling into your routine. Determine a frequency (daily, weekly, etc.) and set aside a specific time for journaling.

- What topics or prompts will you explore in your journal entries?

e. Assessing Current Coping Strategies:

- Reflect on your current coping strategies for anxiety and overthinking in your relationship. Which strategies have been effective? Which ones have been less helpful?

f. Choosing Effective Coping Techniques:

- Select two or three coping strategies from this chapter or elsewhere that resonate with you. Explain why you believe they will be effective in helping you let go of anxiety and overthinking in your relationship.

g. Creating a Daily Coping Routine:

- Outline a daily routine that incorporates your chosen coping strategies. Be specific about when and how you plan to engage in these activities.

- Consider setting reminders or establishing a schedule to help you stay consistent.

h. Tracking Progress and Adjusting Strategies:

- Describe how you will track your progress and evaluate the effectiveness of your coping strategies.

- How will you adjust your coping plan if you find certain strategies are not as helpful as anticipated?

Conclusion

Remember Ariana from the previous chapter? Well, she met a guy named Dan and, employing all they had learned about letting go of anxiety and overthinking in their relationship, they were both able to overcome these challenges and build a beautiful relationship. They eventually had a beautiful wedding, and the lovely Jane was Ariana's maid of honor.

In wrapping up this journey of letting go of anxiety and overthinking in your relationships, it's important to remember that this process is deeply personal and transformative for each of us. Throughout our exploration of coping strategies, we've gained valuable insights into how to navigate and overcome these challenges, and I commend you for your commitment to your wellbeing and that of your relationships.

As we've discovered, self-care and stress management should be at the forefront of your efforts. Prioritizing activities that help you relax and recharge is vital in nurturing your emotional and mental wellbeing. By taking care of yourself, you create a solid foundation from which healthier relationships can grow.

Effective communication techniques are another powerful tool in our journey. Learning to express yourself authentically and openly can reduce misunderstandings and alleviate anxiety. It may take time and practice, but remember that every step you take toward improving your communication skills brings you closer to building more fulfilling connections.

Establishing and reinforcing boundaries is an essential aspect of cultivating healthier relationships. Recognize the areas where you struggle with setting boundaries, and consider the impact it has on your wellbeing. By clearly defining and asserting your boundaries, you create a safe and respectful space for yourself and others.

In the process of decluttering, you embark on a journey to create a more organized and harmonious living space. By letting go of unnecessary belongings, you can create room for clarity and peace in your environment. Decluttering offers an opportunity to assess your possessions and prioritize what truly adds value to your life. As you engage in this process, you will find that decluttering is not just about physical objects but also about letting go of the emotional attachments and mental clutter that can weigh you down.

Throughout this process, don't underestimate the power of seeking support. Trusted individuals who understand and care about you can provide invaluable insights and encouragement. Additionally, remember that professional help is always available if needed. Seeking guidance from therapists or counselors can offer a fresh perspective and support you in your journey of growth.

As you let go of unhealthy safety behaviors, such as excessive worrying or seeking constant reassurance, embrace self-soothing exercises like deep breathing and journaling. These practices allow you to find moments of tranquility and self-reflection, nurturing a deeper understanding of yourself and your emotions.

In conclusion, I want to emphasize that this journey is unique to you. Be patient with yourself and approach it with self-compassion. Commit to incorporating these coping strategies into your life and adapt them to suit your needs. By doing so, you open the door to a more harmonious relationship and personal growth that will be beautiful to see.

Thank You

Thank you so much for purchasing this book.

You could have picked from so many other books, but you took a chance and chose this one.

So, THANK YOU SO MUCH for getting this book and for making it all the way to the end.

Before you go, I wanted to ask you for one small favor. **Could you please consider writing a review on Amazon? Posting a review is the best and easiest way to help other people discover the information in this book and gain true freedom from Overthinning and Relationship Anxiety.**

Your review is very valuable; it will help me to keep writing the kinds of books that will help you get the results you want. I would love to hear from you. Thank you!

>> Leave a review on Amazon US <<

>> Leave a review on Amazon UK <<

References

Abraham, M. (2020). *How anxiety can impair communication.* CalmClinic. Retrieved from https://www.calmclinic.com/anxiety/impairs-communication

Acenda Integrated Health (n.d.). *4 benefits of healthy relationships.* Acenda Integrated Health. Retrieved from https://acendahealth.org/4-benefits-of-healthy-relationships/

Ackerman, C. (2018). *What is neuroplasticity? A psychologist explains [+14 tools].* PositivePsychology. Retrieved from https://positivepsychology.com/neuroplasticity/

American Psychiatric Association. (2013). *Diagnostic and statistical manual of mental disorders (5th ed.).* Washington, DC: American Psychiatric Association.

American Psychiatric Association (2023). *What are anxiety disorders?* Psychiatry.org. Retrieved from https://www.psychiatry.org/patients-families/anxiety-disorders/what-are-anxiety-disorders

American Psychological Association. (n.d.) *Anxiety.* Retrieved from https://www.apa.org/topics/anxiety

Ankrom, S. (2023). *9 breathing exercises to relieve anxiety.* VeryWell Mind. Retrieved from https://www.verywellmind.com/abdominal-breathing-2584115

Anthony (2021). *What are the 5 major types of anxiety disorders?* Mind My Peelings. Retrieved from https://www.mindmypeelings.com/blog/types-of-anxiety

Aronov-Jacoby, S. (2022). *The benefits of self-awareness.* Humber River Health. Retrieved from https://www.hrh.ca/2022/01/27/the-benefits-of-self-awareness/

Bartholomew, K., & Horowitz, L. M. (1991). Attachment styles among young adults: A test of a four-category model. *Journal of Personality and Social Psychology, 61*(2), 226–244. doi:10.1037/0022-3514.61.2.226

Baum, I. (2021). *7 mistakes you're making when trying to get your partner to communicate better.* Well+Good. Retrieved from https://www.wellandgood.com/communication-mistakes-relationships/amp/

Beck, J. S. (2011). *Cognitive behavior therapy: Basics and beyond (2nd ed.).* Guilford Press.

Beckwith, A. & Parkhurst, E. (2022). *The mental benefits of decluttering.* Utah State University, Mental Health Education Extension. Retrieved from https://extension.usu.edu/mentalhealth/articles/the-mental-benefits-of-decluttering

Betz, M. (2022). *What is self-awareness and why is it important?* BetterUp. Retrieved from https://www.betterup.com/blog/what-is-self-awareness

Blue, E. (2018). *Diffusing emotion bombs: Managing anxiety and conflict avoidance in relationships.* Medium. Retrieved from https://medium.com/relationship-by-design/emotional-bomb-diffusion-aa99221a4f1

Burns, D. D. (1999). *Feeling good: The new mood therapy.* Harper Collins.

Caporuscio, J. (2020). *What is relationship anxiety?* Medical News Today. Retrieved from https://www.medicalnewstoday.com/articles/relationship-anxiety

Cassidy, J., & Shaver, P. R. (Eds.) (2016). *Handbook of attachment: Theory, research, and clinical applications (3rd ed.).* Guilford Press.

Cherney, K. (2022). *Effects of anxiety on the body.* Healthline. Retrieved from https://www.healthline.com/health/anxiety/effects-on-body

Cherry, K. (2023). *11 signs of low self-esteem.* VeryWell Mind. Retrieved from https://www.verywellmind.com/signs-of-low-self-esteem

Choy, Y., Fyer, A. J., & Lipsitz, J. D. (2007). Treatment of specific phobia in adults. *Clinical Psychology Review, 27*(3), 266–286. doi:10.1016/j.cpr.2006.10.002

Christopher, F. S., & Cate, R. M. (2018). Gender roles, power, and relationships. In T. D. Fisher, C. M. Davis, W. L. Yarber, & S. L. Davis (Eds.), *Handbook of Quality-Related Measures* (4th ed., pp. 447–454). Routledge.

Chukuemeka, E. S. (2022). *Effects of overthinking on your mental, emotional, and physical health.* Bscholarly. Retrieved from https://bscholarly.com/effects-of-overthinking/

Clark, D. A., & Beck, A. T. (2010). *Cognitive therapy of anxiety disorders: Science and practice.* Guilford Press.

Cleveland Clinic (2021). *How to do a digital detox for less stress, and more focus.* Cleveland Clinic Health Essentials. Retrieved from https://health.clevelandclinic.org/digital-detox/

Cloitre, M., Stolbach, B. C., Herman, J. L., Van der Kolk, B., Pynoos, R., Wang, J., & Petkova, E. (2009). A developmental approach to complex PTSD: Childhood and adult cumulative trauma as predictors of symptom complexity. *Journal of Traumatic Stress, 22*(5), 399–408. doi:10.1002/jts.20444

Colino, S. (2022). *Why decluttering is important for self-care (and when it isn't)*. Everyday Health. Retrieved from https://www.everydayhealth.com/healthy-living/why-decluttering-is-important-for-self-care-and-when-it-isnt/

Cuncic, A. (2023). *Negative thoughts: How to stop them*. VeryWell Mind. Retrieved from https://www.verywellmind.com/how-to-change-negative-thinking-3024843

Daisy (2020). *What is mental clutter? (And how to clear it)*. Simple Not Stressful. Retrieved from https://simplenotstressful.com/blog/mental-clutter

Davidson, R. J., & McEwen, B. S. (2012). Social influences on neuroplasticity: Stress and interventions to promote well-being. *Nature Neuroscience, 15*(5), 689–695. doi:10.1038/nn.3093

Davis, K. (2023). *How does cognitive behavioral therapy work?* Medical News Today. Retrieved from https://www.medicalnewstoday.com/articles/296579

Delap, D. (2022). *The physical effects of clutter on your brain and body*. Psychology Today. Retrieved from https://www.psychologytoday.com/us/blog/minding-your-mess/202207/the-physical-effects-clutter-your-brain-and-body

DeMartini, J., Patel, G., & Fancher, T. L. (2019). Generalized anxiety disorder. *Annals of Internal Medicine, 170*(7), ITC49–ITC64. doi:10.7326/AITC201904020

DPS Staff (2021). *10 ways to practice self-talk*. Delaware Psychological Services. Retrieved from https://www.delawarepsychologicalservices.com/post/10-ways-to-practice-positive-self-talk

Ein-Dor, T., Mikulincer, M., Doron, G., & Shaver, P. R. (2015). The attachment paradox: How can so many of us (the insecure ones) have no adaptive advantages? *Perspectives on Psychological Science, 10*(6), 665–685. doi:10.1177/1745691610362349

Eisenberg, N., Cumberland, A., & Spinrad, T. L. (1998). Parental socialization of emotion. *Psychological Inquiry, 9*(4), 241–273. doi:10.1207/s15327965pli0904_1

Eisler, M. (2019). *15 ways to declutter your mind*. Chopra. Retrieved from

https://chopra.com/articles/15waystodeclutteryourmind

Feeney, J. A., & Noller, P. (1990). Attachment style as a predictor of adult romantic relationships. *Journal of Personality and Social Psychology, 58*(2), 281–291. doi:10.1037/0022-3514.58.2.281

Feiring, C., & Taska, L. (2005). The persistence of shame following sexual abuse: A longitudinal look at risk and recovery. *Child Maltreatment, 10*(4), 337–349. doi:10.1177/1077559505276686

Feyoh, M. (2023). *29 journaling prompts for anxiety help in 2023*. Happier Human. Retrieved from https://www.happierhuman.com/journaling-prompts-anxiety/

Firestone, L. (2020). *Forgiveness: The secret to a healthy relationship*. PsychAlive. Retrieved from https://www.psychalive.org/forgiveness-the-secret-to-a-healthy-relationship/

Goldin, P. R., & Gross, J. J. (2010). Effects of mindfulness-based stress reduction (MBSR) on emotion regulation in social anxiety disorder. *Emotion, 10*(1), 83–91. doi:10.1037/a0018441

Gonsalves, K. (2023). *The 4 attachment styles in relationships + how to find yours*. MindBodyGreen. Retrieved from https://www.mindbodygreen.com/articles/attachment-theory-and-the-4-attachment-styles

Grossman, D. (2018). *The art of active listening*. The Grossman Group. Retrieved from https://www.yourthoughtpartner.com/blog/the-art-of-active-listening

Hall, J. (2020). *10 habits to keep your relationships strong*. Forbes. Retrieved from https://www.forbes.com/sites/johnhall/2020/05/31/10hab itstokeepyourrelationshipsstrong/amp/

Hayes, S. C., Strosahl, K. D., & Wilson, K. G. (2012). *Acceptance and commitment therapy: The process and practice of mindful change (2nd ed.).* Guilford Press.

High Focus Treatment Centers (2021). *Learning to challenge negative thoughts.* High Focus Treatment Centers. Retrieved from https://www.highfocuscenters.com/learning-to-challenge-negative-thoughts/

Hofmann, S. G. (2011). *An introduction to modern CBT: Psychological solutions to mental health problems.* John Wiley & Sons.

Holland, K. (2022). *Everything you need to know about anxiety.* Healthline. Retrieved from https://www.healthline.com/health/anxiety

Holland, K. (2020). *Positive self-talk: how talking to yourself is a good thing.* Healthline. Retrieved from https://www.healthline.com/health/positive-self-talk

Hoshaw, C. (2022). *What is mindfulness? A simple practice for greater wellbeing.* Healthline. Retrieved from https://www.healthline.com/health/mind-body/what-is-mindfulness

Howard, T. (2021). *The importance of showing gratitude to your partner.* Utah State University, Relationships Extension. Retrieved from https://extension.usu.edu/relationships/faq/the-importance-of-showing-gratitude-to-your-partner

Hutchinson, A. (2022). *What is graded exposure therapy?* Ovrcome.io. Retrieved from https://www.ovrcome.io/amp/what-is-graded-exposure-therapy

Ivory, D. (2022). *How to practice mindfulness in daily life.* Mindful. Retrieved from https://www.mindful.org/mindfulness-how-to-do-it/

Iyarn (2020). *Vulnerability for building stronger connections.* Iyarn. Retrieved from https://iyarn.com/blog/vulnerability-building-stronger-connections/

Izuakam, J. (2023). *What is your attachment style?* The Guardian: Life. Retrieved from https://guardian.ng/life/what-is-your-attachment-style/

Jenna (2023). *What is mental clutter and how can you reduce it?* Tidymalism. Retrieved from https://tidymalism.com/what-is-mental-clutter/

Johansson, R., Andersson, G., & Paxling, B. (2012). A randomized controlled trial of internet-based cognitive behavior therapy, self-help booklet, and no treatment for social anxiety disorder in Japan. *Cognitive Behaviour Therapy, 41*(2), 106–116.

Katz, L. F., & Windecker-Nelson, B. (2004). Parental meta-emotion philosophy in families with conduct-problem children: Links with peer relations. *Journal of Abnormal Child Psychology, 32*(4), 385–398. doi:10.1023/b:jacp.0000030292.36168.30

Kendler, K. S., Eaves, L. J., Loken, E. K., Pedersen, N. L., Middeldorp, C. M., Reynolds, C., Boomsma, D., Lichtenstein, P., Silberg, J., & Gardner, C. O. (2011). The impact of environmental experiences on symptoms of anxiety and depression across the life span. *Psychological Science, 22*(10), 1343–1352. doi:10.1177/0956797611417255

Keng, S. L., Smoski, M. J., & Robins, C. J. (2011). Effects of mindfulness on psychological health: A review of empirical studies. *Clinical Psychology Review, 31*(6), 1041–1056. doi:10.1016/j.cpr.2011.04.006

Knight, A. (2023). *Why overthinking is bad for your health? – Insomnia, anxiety, depression & decreased productivity.* Fischer Institute. Retrieved from https://fischerinstitute.com/overthinking-is-bad-for-health/

Knobloch-Westerwick, S., & Alter, S. (2017). Idealized media images and women's satisfaction with their relationships: Perceiving high idealized media images negatively predicts satisfaction. *Communication Research, 44*(5), 672–696.

Kumar, V. K. (2023). *Attachment theory.* StatPearls Publishing.

Lebow, I. H. (2021). *6 neuroplasticity exercises for anxiety relief.* Psych Central. Retrieved from https://psychcentral.com/anxiety/how-to-train-your-brain-to-alleviate-anxiety

Leonard, A. (2022). The impact of trauma on mental health. *Journal of Trauma and Recovery, 10*(2), 123–145.

Leonard, J. (2020). *What is trauma? What to know.* Medical News Today. Retrieved from https://www.medicalnewstoday.com/articles/trauma

Lindberg, S. (2021). *What are the types of anxiety disorders?* Healthline. Retrieved from https://www.healthline.com/health/anxiety/types-of-anxiety

Lindberg, S. (2023). *How does your environment affect your mental health?* VeryWell Mind. Retrieved from https://www.verywellmind.com/how-your-environment-affects-your-mental-health

Lok, A., Frijling, J. L., & van Zuiden, M. (2018). Posttraumatic stress disorder: Current insights in diagnostics, treatment and prevention. *Ned Tijdschr Geneeskd, 161*(3), D1905.

Los Angeles Christian Counseling. (2020). *16 characteristics of a happy couple.* LA Christian Counseling. Retrieved from https://lachristiancounseling.com/articles/16-characteristics-of-a-happy-couple

Madison, R. (2020). *6 exercises to strengthen emotional intimacy in your marriage.* First Things First. Retrieved from https://firstthings.org/strengthen-emotional-intimacy-in-marriage/

Mandriota, M. (2022). *All about the cycle of anxiety: What it is and how to cope.* Psych Central. Retrieved from https://psychcentral.com/anxiety/cycle-of-anxiety

Mantell, M. (n.d). *Vulnerability exercises to get more fulfilling relationships.* Mike Mantell. Retrieved from https://mikemantell.com/vulnerability-exercises/

Markowicz, J. (2021). *Attachment styles and hope for your relationship.* GoodTherapy Blog. Retrieved from https://www.goodtherapy.org/blog/Attachment-Styles-Hope-for-Your-Relationship

Mayo Clinic Staff. (2019). *Social anxiety disorder (social phobia).* Mayo Clinic. Retrieved from https://www.mayoclinic.org/diseases-conditions/social-anxiety-disorder/symptoms-causes/syc-20353561

McDermott, N. (2023). *What are the attachment styles—and how can they impact your relationship?* Forbes Health. Retrieved from https://www.forbes.com/health/mind/what-are-the-attachment-styles/

McLean, K. (2021). *Understanding codependency (anxious attachment).* Kennedy McLean Counselling & Psychotherapy Services. Retrieved from https://www.kennedymclean.com/amp/understanding-codependency-anxious-attachment

Mental Health Foundation (2022). *Anxiety.* Mental Health Foundation. Retrieved from https://www.mentalhealth.org.uk/a-to-z/a/anxiety

Mental Health Foundation (2022). *Physical health and mental health.* Mental Health Foundation. Retrieved from https://www.mentalhealth.org.uk/explore-mental-health/a-z-topics/physical-health-and-mental-health

Mikulincer, M., & Shaver, P. R. (2016). *Attachment in adulthood: Structure, dynamics, and change (2nd ed.).* Guilford Press.

Mind (2021). *Anxiety and panic attacks.* Mind. Retrieved from https://www.mind.org.uk/information-support/types-of-mental-health-problems/anxiety-and-panic-attacks/

Morin, A. (2023). *How to stop overthinking.* VeryWell Mind.
Retrieved from https://www.verywellmind.com/how-to-
know-when-youre-overthinking-5077069

Morris, Y. S. (2016). *What are the benefits of self-talk?*
Healthline. Retrieved from
https://www.healthline.com/health/mental-health/self-talk

Nash, J. (2022). *24 best self-soothing techniques and strategies
for adults.* Positive Psychology. Retrieved from
https://positivepsychology.com/self-soothing/

National Health Service (2022). *Overview - Cognitive
Behavioural Therapy (CBT).* NHS. Retrieved from
https://www.nhs.uk/mental-health/talking-therapies-
medicine-treatments/talking-therapies-and-
counselling/cognitive-behavioural-therapy-cbt/overview/

National Health Service (2023). *Post-traumatic stress disorder
(PTSD).* NHS Inform. Retrieved from
https://www.nhsinform.scot/illnesses-and-
conditions/mental-health/post-traumatic-stress-disorder-
ptsd

National Institute on Aging (2020). *5 tips for dealing with
social anxiety as you age.* Retrieved from
https://www.nia.nih.gov/news/social-anxiety-tips

National Institute of Mental Health (2023). *Anxiety disorders.*
NIMH. Retrieved from

https://www.nimh.nih.gov/health/topics/anxiety-disorders/index.shtml

Nazish, N. (2017). *How to declutter your mind: 10 practical tips you'll actually want to try*. Forbes. Retrieved from https://www.forbes.com/sites/nomanazish/2017/11/19/how-to-declutter-your-mind-10-practical-tips-youll-actually-want-to-try/?sh=145fba0f24f1

Newman, M. G., & Llera, S. J. (2011). A novel theory of experiential avoidance in generalized anxiety disorder: A review and synthesis of research supporting a contrast avoidance model of worry. *Clinical Psychology Review, 31*(3), 371–382. doi:10.1016/j.cpr.2011.01.008

Nwokolo, C. (2022). *5 damaging health effects of overthinking*. HealthGuide. Retrieved from https://healthguide.ng/health-effects-of-overthinking/

Pattemore, C. (2021). *How to set boundaries in your relationships*. Psych Central. Retrieved from https://psychcentral.com/blog/why-healthy-relationships-always-have-boundaries-how-to-set-boundaries-in-yours

Peterson, T. (2015). *Anxiety and overthinking everything*. Healthy Place. Retrieved from https://www.healthyplace.com/blogs/anxiety-schmanxiety/2015/12/anxiety-and-over-thinking-everything

Peterson, T. (2018). *Safety behaviors with social anxiety: Helpful or harmful?* Healthy Place. Retrieved from https://www.healthyplace.com/blogs/anxiety-schmanxiety/2018/7/safety-behaviors-with-social-anxiety-helpful-or-harmful

Phelps, B. (2020). *10 benefits of happy relationships.* WebMD. Retrieved from https://blogs.webmd.com/relationships/20200715/10-benefits-of-happy-relationships

Pietrangelo, A. (2023). *How to be happy: 27 habits to add to your routine.* Healthline. Retrieved from https://www.healthline.com/health/how-to-be-happy/

Pinnacle Recovery (2019). *What are the 4 R's of anxiety?* Pinnacle Recovery. Retrieved from https://pinnaclerecoveryut.com/what-are-the-4-rs-of-anxiety/

Poplin, J. (2022). *Decluttering & self-care: The benefits of letting go.* The Simplicity Habit. Retrieved from https://www.thesimplicityhabit.com/decluttering-and-self-care-the-benefits-of-letting-go/

Powell, A. (2022). *Relationship anxiety: Signs, causes, & 8 ways to overcome.* Choosing Therapy. Retrieved from https://www.choosingtherapy.com/relationship-anxiety/

Qhek, J. (2022). *The truth behind safety behaviours*. Chill By Nette. Retrieved from https://chillbynette.com/the-truth-behind-safety-behaviours/

Rapee, R. M., & Heimberg, R. G. (1997). A cognitive-behavioral model of anxiety in social phobia. *Behaviour Research and Therapy, 35*(8), 741–756. doi:10.1016/S0005-7967(97)00022-3

Ray, S. (2023). *Conflict resolution: Process, strategies & skills*. Project Manager. Retrieved from https://www.projectmanager.com/blog/conflict-resolution-strategies

Reid, S. (2023). *Setting healthy boundaries in relationships*. HelpGuide. Retrieved from https://www.helpguide.org/articles/relationships-communication/setting-healthy-boundaries-in-relationships.htm

Richards, L. (2022). *What is positive self-talk?* Medical News Today. Retrieved from https://www.medicalnewstoday.com/articles/positive-self-talk

Robbins, T. (2023). *Why do I overthink everything?* Tony Robbins. Retrieved from https://www.tonyrobbins.com/mental-health/how-to-stop-overthinking/

Robinson, L., Segal, J., & Jaffe, J. (2023). *How attachment styles affect adult relationships.* HelpGuide. Retrieved from https://www.helpguide.org/articles/relationships-communication/attachment-and-adult-relationships.htm

Rodriguez, L. M., DiBello, A. M., Øverup, C. S., & Neighbors, C. (2015). The price of distrust: Trust, anxious attachment, jealousy, and partner abuse. *Partner Abuse, 6*(3), 298–319. doi:10.1891/1946-6560.6.3.298

Roncero, A. (2021). *Automatic thoughts: How to identify and fix them.* BetterUp Blog. Retrieved from https://www.betterup.com/blog/automatic-thoughts

Rosenbaum, S., Tiedemann, A., Sherrington, C., Curtis, J., & Ward, P. B. (2014). Physical activity interventions for people with mental illness: A systematic review and meta-analysis. *Journal of Clinical Psychiatry, 75*(9), 964–974. doi:10.4088/JCP.13r08765

Ryder, G. (2022). *What is trauma?* Psych Central. Retrieved from https://psychcentral.com/health/what-is-trauma

Salaky, K. (2017). 9 surprising benefits of being in a good relationship. *Insider.* Retrieved from https://www.insider.com/health-benefits-of-being-in-a-relationship-dating-someone-2017-10

Schwartz, B. (2022). *Self-soothing: What it is, benefits, & techniques to get started.* Choosing Therapy. Retrieved from https://www.choosingtherapy.com/self-soothing/

Scolan, D. (2021). *Rumination.* The OCD & Anxiety Center. Retrieved from https://theocdandanxietycenter.com/rumination/

Segrin, C., & Flora, J. (2011). *Family communication (2nd ed.).* Routledge.

Sharma, S. (2022). *6 simple neuroplasticity exercises to rewire your anxious brain.* Calm Sage. Retrieved from https://www.calmsage.com/neuroplasticity-exercises/

Shea, M. (2021). *Try greeting your anxiety with the 4 Rs.* Shine. Retrieved from https://advice.theshineapp.com/articles/try-greeting-your-anxiety-with-the-4rs/

Simpson, J. A., Collins, W. A., Tran, S., & Haydon, K. C. (2007). Attachment and the experience and expression of emotions in romantic relationships: A developmental perspective. *Journal of Personality and Social Psychology, 92*(2), 355–367. doi:10.1037/0022-3514.92.2.355

Smith, S. (2021). *20 benefits of healthy relationships.* Marriage.com. Retrieved from https://www.marriage.com/advice/relationship/benefits-of-healthy-relationships/

Smith, S. (2021). *How important is intimacy in a relationship?* Marriage.com. Retrieved from https://www.marriage.com/advice/intimacy/how-important-is-intimacy-in-a-relationship/

Smith, S. (2021). *The importance of communication in relationships.* Marriage.com. Retrieved from https://www.marriage.com/advice/communication/importance-of-communication-in-relationships/

Soken-Huberty, E. (2023). *10 reasons why self-awareness is important.* The Important Site. Retrieved from https://theimportantsite.com/10-reasons-why-self-awareness-is-important/

Solvere Living. (2023). *Six ways to declutter your mind mentally and emotionally.* Solvere Living. Retrieved from https://solvereliving.com/blog/six-ways-to-declutter-your-mind-mentally-and-emotionally/

Spielberger, C. D. (1972). *Anxiety: Current trends in theory and research.* Academic Press.

Stanborough, J. R. (2020). *How to change negative thinking with cognitive restructuring.* Healthline. Retrieved from https://www.healthline.com/health/cognitive-restructuring

Stress & Development Lab, Harvard University. *Identifying negative thought patterns.* Harvard University. Retrieved from https://sdlab.fas.harvard.edu/cognitive-reappraisal/identifying-negative-automatic-thought-patterns

Stritof, S. (2022). *How to deal with jealousy in a relationship.* VeryWell Mind. Retrieved from https://www.verywellmind.com/overcome-jealousy-in-your-marriage-2303979

Sugden, L. (2022). *7 neuroplasticity exercises to rewire your brain.* Heights. Retrieved from https://www.yourheights.com/blog/health/neuroplasticity-exercises/

Swaby, M. (2019). *12 ways to recognize negative thoughts.* Benevolent Health. Retrieved from https://benevolenthealth.co.uk/12-ways-to-recognise-negative-thoughts/

Szymanski, D. M., & Kashubeck-West, S. (2014). Mediators of the relationship between social support and well-being in Latina breast cancer survivors. *Journal of Counseling Psychology, 61*(3), 358–369.

Thompson, J. (2022). *9 neuroplasticity exercises to boost productivity.* WorkLife. Retrieved from https://www.atlassian.com/blog/productivity/neuroplasticity-train-your-brain/

Toshi N. (2023). *Overthinking – To what extent can it damage your life?* PharmEasy. Retrieved from https://pharmeasy.in/blog/overthinking-to-what-extent-can-it-damage-your-life/

Tuca, A. (2023). *16 digital detox tips that actually work in 2023*. ThemeIsle. Retrieved from https://themeisle.com/blog/digital-detox-tips/

Van Overbeek, G., & Scholte, R. H. (2007). Effects of a cognitive-behavioral self-help program and a computerized structured writing intervention on depressed mood for Internet-based self-help coping with bereavement. *CyberPsychology & Behavior, 10*(6), 845–851.

Vidakovic, F. (2023). *50 journal prompts for anxiety – To feel less anxious*. Inspiring Life. Retrieved from https://www.inspiringmomlife.com/journal-prompts-for-anxiety/

Walters, M. (2022). *10 healthy habits that should be a priority in your marriage*. The Dating Divas. Retrieved from https://www.thedatingdivas.com/10-healthy-habits-that-should-be-a-priority-in-your-marriage/

WebMD Editorial Contributors. (2023). *Anxiety disorders*. WebMD. Retrieved from https://www.webmd.com/anxiety-panic/guide/anxiety-disorders

Wegner, D. M. (1994). Ironic processes of mental control. *Psychological Review, 101*(1), 34–52. doi:10.1037/0033-295X.101.1.34

Whelan, C. (2022). *How to manage low self-esteem.* Healthline. Retrieved from https://www.healthline.com/health/low-self-esteem

Witmer, S. (2023). *What is overthinking, and how do i stop overthinking everything?* GoodRx Health. Retrieved from https://www.goodrx.com/health-topic/mental-health/how-can-i-stop-overthinking-everything

Woods, E. (2021). *How your partner's past relationships & partners affect you.* Pure Health Center. Retrieved from https://purehealthcenter.com/how-your-partners-past-relationships-partners-affect-you/

Zaki, J., & Williams, W. C. (2013). Interpersonal emotion regulation. *Emotion, 13*(5), 803–810. doi:10.1037/a0033839

Printed in Great Britain
by Amazon

43201494R00145